M000079149

THE SPORT OF SCHOOL

THE SPORT OF SCHOOL

OF SCHOOL

HELP YOUR STUDENT-ATHLETE WIN IN THE CLASSROOM

CHRISTIAN K. BUCK

LIONCREST
PUBLISHING

COPYRIGHT © 2020 CHRISTIAN K. BUCK

All rights reserved.

THE SPORT OF SCHOOL

Help Your Student-Athlete Win in the Classroom

ISBN   978-1-5445-1606-6 *Hardcover*

        978-1-5445-1605-9 *Paperback*

        978-1-5445-1604-2 *Ebook*

This book is dedicated to my son, Jack, and to all the students of the world who are passionate about improving their performance and driven to being the best they can be.

CONTENTS

PART ONE: PREGAME

PART TWO: GAME ON!

PREGAME

CHAPTER 1

FORMING A GAME PLAN TO MOTIVATE STUDENT-ATHLETES

"Don't let him waste his money on the application."

That was the dean of admissions' response when my college counselor contacted him about my potential future of playing lacrosse at his school. He rejected me before he even received my application.

That was the summer before my senior year in high school. It was a sobering experience. I suddenly realized how poorly I measured up to my classmates—my class rank was 205 out of 275. Not good.

Though painful, it was a pivotal moment in my life. Without that kick in the ass, I wouldn't have recognized the need to change my habits. I decided then and there that I was going to completely transform how I approached my academics.

I wrote that dean a letter stating that I was determined to improve my grades and get into his school. After receiving a 2.8 GPA during my first three years of high school, I improved to a 3.8 during my senior year. I didn't get smarter that semester; I just tried for the first time.

And that's the point of my practice and this book. My job is to get students to change how they see school—to really try, maybe for the first time, and to work harder and smarter. To take the effort they exert on the field and translate it into the classroom—in other words, to treat school like a sport.

If your son or daughter isn't living up to their potential right now, this book is for you. I can say confidently that this Sport of School approach absolutely works. The experience varies with each unique individual, but the results are the same. In the ten years I've worked as a mental conditioning coach and performance expert, consulting students on academic improvement, the GPAs of more than one hundred clients have improved from an average of 2.8 to an average of 3.5.

So, here comes the cold water: The landscape of the college admissions process has changed. It's *much* more competitive to get into an elite college than it was when you and I were growing up. Almost without exception, friends, colleagues, and peers tell me they never would have gotten into the college they attended if they were to apply today—and, they're probably right. The acceptance rates for top colleges and universities have dropped; therefore, the importance of high school grades has increased. Today, more kids are applying and competing for the same number of postsecondary spots.

According to Vinay Bhaskara, co-founder of Massachusetts-based CollegeVine, which provides college admissions guidance, "The pressure is most acute at the top universities. Having a college degree in America has gone from nice-to-have to something you need-to- have for even a lower-middle-class life in American society today."[1]

The number of spots available has become more limited. What's more, the overall enrollment of young adults at postsecondary institutions has grown from 25% in 1970 to 40% in 2014, according to the National Center for Education Statistics, and this has meant lower acceptance rates. In 1990, the acceptance rate at the University of Pennsylvania was 41%, but *U.S. News & World Report* listed an acceptance rate of just 10% in 2017.[2]

1   Powell, Farran. "How Competitive Is College Admissions?" *U.S. News & World Report*, 22 Sept. 2016, www.usnews.com/education/best-colleges/ articles/2016-09-22/ how-competitive-is-college-admissions.

2   Compass, U.S. News College, and Read the Best Colleges Methodology. "The 10 Best Universities in America." *U.S. News & World Report*,, www. usnews.com/best-colleges/rankings/ national-universities.

State schools remain some of the most competitive institutions in the country, even more so if you want to attend one outside of your state. The University of North Carolina, for example, accepts only 18% of its incoming freshman from out of state. This policy reflects UNC's desire to serve state residents first and foremost, thus causing a ripple effect for any students living outside of North Carolina. According to Stephen Farmer, vice provost for enrollment and undergraduate admissions, while the in-state acceptance rate has hovered around 50% for the last ten years, the out-of-state acceptance rate has now dropped below 20%.

There is also a misunderstanding in the ranks of high school sports that distracts many student-athletes. It's commonplace to believe that if student-athletes are good enough at their sport, they will be offered a full athletic scholarship. In actuality, the odds of earning an athletic scholarship are miniscule. According to *CBS News*, only about 2% of all high school seniors earn a college athletic scholarship each year. For those who do, the average scholarship is less than $11,000.[3] Meanwhile, Ivy League and NCAA Division III schools do not offer any athletic scholarships.

The NCAA estimates that only 6.7% of 1,083,617 high school football players will play football in college. Fur-

---

3   O'Shaughnessy, Lynn. "8 Things You Should Know about Sports Scholarships." *CBS News*, CBS Interactive, 20 Sept. 2012, www.cbsnews.com/news/8-things-you-should- know-about-sports-scholarships/.

thermore, only 1.6% of college football players will play in the NFL. Obviously, the odds of going pro are extremely small. What if your student-athlete has chosen to run track, swim, or fence? What are the chances of playing that sport professionally as his or her sole source of income? It seems the odds are so low that the NCAA doesn't even track those statistics.

Due to the low odds of making it to the next level of college or professional sports, we must recognize the need to prepare our student-athletes for college without sports, and for life in general.

Students can often feel a tremendous amount of pressure to attend the "right" college to earn their degree. They are bombarded by daily messages, both inside of the home and out, convincing them that only the best schools are valid options. This pressure manifests itself in high levels of anxiety: if they don't attend a "good" school, it will be seen as a failure. Imagine that weight on your shoulders every day.

Due to the increased competition in admissions, high school students and their families have turned to college counselors and tutors in record numbers. According to Mark Sklarow, executive director at the Independent Educational Consultants Association, at least a quarter of students bound for private colleges or out-of-state schools use a personal college counselor. As for tutors, Global

Industry Analysts, Inc., released a study stating that the global private tutoring market is projected to surpass $227 billion by 2022, of which the United States accounts for 90%.[4]

The use of tutors and private college counselors has industrialized the process of getting good grades, and although tutors and counselors have helped countless students, this is not a holistic approach. Due to this new competitive environment and the pressure to perform, *grades* have become the focal point of school, not the *education* students receive.

PRIORITIZING EFFORT OVER RESULTS

Grades are the *outcome* of a process. Just as a low golf score is the outcome of good coaching and hours and hours of practice, grades represent the final outcome of the effort, focus, intensity, and practice put into each assignment.

Today, a student's grades designate what institutions they may be able to attend. Good or bad, they are part of an individual's résumé, or what I call a student's *marketing plan.* In high school, grades are regarded as a means to an end: get the best grades possible, to get into the best college possible, to get the best job possible, and so on. But we have to ask ourselves, "Is our goal to prepare our students for the next

---

4   Private Tutoring: A Global Strategic Business Report. Global Industry Analysts Inc, 5 Oct. 2016, www.strategyr.com/pressMCP-1597.asp.

four years or the next forty?" If students are to succeed in the long term, we need to change the paradigm of how we motivate them.

We need to switch from forcing students to improve their grades because we demand it, to motivating them to strive for success on their own. If we recognize their motivation—not the grades themselves—as the key to improvement, then that's what we should address. Not only will students improve their grades, but they will also be able to apply that motivation to any aspect of their lives. By taking control of their academic performance and charting their own course, they are fueled not only by the knowledge and competency that comes with a good education, but also by a feeling of personal accomplishment.

How do we get that message across to our kids? It's easy enough to say, but harder to do. My approach is to look at the characteristics that make a great athlete and help student-athletes apply those characteristics in the classroom:

- **Focus:** Great athletes are able to focus on the task at hand and tune out distractions.
- **Drive:** Great athletes are driven to improve every day. They are not satisfied with their last performance.
- **Discipline:** Great athletes are disciplined enough to stay on strict schedules; for example, adhering to eating or exercise programs.

- **Determination:** Great athletes never give up, no matter how challenging the situation may be. They quickly bounce back from setbacks or failure.
- **Commitment:** Great athletes are committed to their sport. It is not a "sometimes" thing.
- **Vision:** Great athletes have a clear vision of what they want to accomplish and how to do it.
- **Aggressiveness:** Great athletes make moves on their own. They do not simply respond to what other athletes do.

Everyone generally understands what makes a great athlete. What's less obvious is what makes a great student. However, if we were to write a list of characteristics that make a great student, the list would look exactly the same.

In short, the goal of this book—and the Sport of School Model—is to take what we know about *athletic* performance and apply it to *human* performance, and more specifically to *academic* performance. If students become intrinsically motivated and learn to value hard work, grit, perseverance, and continual learning, they can navigate the road to success on their own. We preach these values from the sidelines and on the ride home from practice: why don't we apply them to school?

This book is organized into two parts. In Part 1, "Pregame," we'll discuss some background information about work ethic, motivation, and how different student-athletes approach sports and school:

- In Chapter 2, we'll discuss how work ethic is something that can be learned and consider ways you can help your child improve her work ethic by being the motorboat that creates waves, rather than the cork that bobs along without direction.
- One of the key principles in this model is that motivation to change must come from your student-athlete, not you. Chapter 3 will help you understand your child's needs and what motivates him so you can meet your child right where he is.
- Chapter 4 presents five student-athlete types, along with ways to help each type improve academic performance.

In Part 2, "Game On!" I'll cover the Sport of School Model in detail:

- Chapter 5 presents an overview of the Sport of School Model. The next three chapters focus on the three key elements:
  - Understanding consequences (Chapter 6)
  - Recognizing lifetime goals (Chapter 7)
  - Deciding versus committing to change (Chapter 8)
- Chapter 9 discusses one of the major roadblocks student-athletes encounter: self-doubt.

Throughout the book, you'll read first-person stories from clients whose academic performance—and more importantly, their lives after college—changed by following this model (names have been changed to protect their identities). My hope is that you will share these stories with your student-athlete to spark a new way of thinking as she learns from someone who has already achieved success using this model. I also hope these stories will help you open a dialogue with your child about implementing his own new mindset toward school.

APPLYING SPORT PSYCHOLOGY CONCEPTS TO ACADEMICS

Let's go back to my story, when I improved my GPA from 2.8 to 3.8. At the time, it occurred to me that I was putting hours of practice into improving my lacrosse skills, and that if I just approached school in the same way, I would see the same results. For the first time, I had a plan—and more importantly, a vision—for my future. Even though my post–high school future didn't start at the college to which I had wanted to apply, I did get accepted to an academically equivalent school. Because I turned my grades around, I was able to fulfill my dream of playing goalie at the college level. It was stressful and pressure-filled, but I loved it.

I also continued to make an effort in the classroom and I did well in college. After graduation, I spent eleven years trading and brokering equity derivatives on the floor of the American Stock Exchange, and then I started a brokerage. If you think trading your own money is nerve-wracking, try trading someone else's. That role carried a whole new level of stress and pressure. As you can imagine, the clients on the other end of the phone were not the Boy Scouts. This was a dog-eat-dog world. Add to that the ever-present ominous feeling that came with working in downtown Manhattan after 9/11. The stress finally came to a head one morning when I experienced a panic attack on the subway going into work. Something had to change.

I sold my portion of the brokerage, took a leap of faith, and went back to school full time to earn my master's in sports psychology. At age thirty-five, sports psychology became my life. Grad school was my new full-time job.

In grad school, I tried to get as much education and experience as I could, working with numerous athletes in a wide array of sports. I coached a local high school girls' lacrosse team, and I interned in the mental conditioning department of IMG Academies, working with some of the best young athletes in the country. I got certified to teach Fearless Golf, the process of mental skills training developed by Dr. Gio Valiante, who works with many of the best golfers in the world. I even consulted with one of the world's best long drive competitors (if you want to feel bad about your golf drive, go work with one of those guys).

After grad school, a friend asked if I would like to be an assistant coach. He had recently become the head coach of a nationally ranked high school boys' lacrosse team. I jumped at the chance. Not only could I assist the team as a coach, but I could also help the players prepare mentally. Working with this team formed the genesis of the Sport of School Model.

During my work with students over the past ten years, I have realized that it is possible for almost any student to see better results (and by "results" I mean dramatic academic improvement) or at the very least an increase in the amount of effort regarding schoolwork. Not everyone has to earn a 3.8 GPA in order to consider my model a success.

When students change their perspective toward school and treat it as a sport, they see dramatic changes. After seeing these improvements in over one hundred clients, I decided to write this book to help as many students (and parents) as I can.

In this book, I will share how students have changed their lives by developing this Sport of School mindset—how they went from seeing school as a chore to seeing it in the same vein as sports. This mindset is a tool they can use to fine-tune their skills and set themselves up for success.

With your help, I want to inspire students to break through

their self-created limitations and take control of their academic performance and their future. I want to demonstrate to parents, coaches, and teachers what I have learned about how students approach school and that it is possible to redirect students' ambivalent attitude toward academics into a powerful mindset.

That might sound like a daunting task, but I will take you through my approach step by step so you can gain a practical understanding of how to help your own student-athlete improve in school. I will also show you how to apply that knowledge using some of my most successful practices.

While I recognize that learning and work ethic are the keys to long-term success, we can't dismiss grades entirely. Earning better grades will affect students' options when considering potential colleges, but the college they attend doesn't necessarily predict future success (as I tell my clients: success is not the bumper sticker on your parent's car).

At times, my message may seem contradictory: Grades are important. Grades are not important. Please recognize that my intent is to help students improve their grades, but the ancillary benefits of better grades—like higher self-esteem and learning the value of a strong work ethic—are the ultimate goals and the greatest reward. Please join me in helping students become their greatest selves and finally reach the potential we all know they have.

THE ROLE OF THE COACH

So far, I've been talking about the student-athlete, but as in sports, coaching can play a critical role in academic success. The role of a coach in athletics is relatively clear, and parents must play a similar role in improving their student's academic life. If you have ever coached your kid's youth baseball or basketball team, you know how difficult it can be to coach your own child. It requires empathy, patience, and persistence. It also requires giving athletes control and empowering their decision-making. Coaching your child in academics is no different.

If you're reading this book, you may have already tried the first tools most parents reach for when trying to improve their student's grades: rewarding good grades with money or privileges or punishing poor grades by taking away those privileges. If that's true, you are likely frustrated, even exasperated, by your child's apparent apathy. But I'm here to tell you that through empathy and the techniques outlined in this book, you can achieve breakthroughs. That's what a coach does: finds the plays and strategies that work best for the team and helps athletes to reach their potential.

As a mental conditioning coach and expert in performance, I consider myself part of a student's coaching staff, along with his or her parents. Depending on your child's physical and mental challenges and needs, you may decide to invite other types of professionals to join your "staff."

For example, while I have a master's degree in sports psychology, it's important to note that I am not a licensed psychologist. The term "psychology" is protected by law and refers to the licensed practice of psychology. When working with athletes, this largely refers to mental health counseling or clinical psychology. Professionals licensed in this field have extensive academic and supervised experience working with people who struggle with depression, eating disorders, anxiety disorders, and attention deficit disorders. If your child wrestles with these more serious issues, you may wish to interview professionals to specifically address those conditions, which affect all aspects of life, not just academic performance.

Most parents who come to me are frustrated that nothing appears to be wrong from a clinical standpoint, yet their student simply doesn't appear to care and can't be motivated to prioritize academics. I can definitely help with that.

This approach can work with any student, not just athletes. There are many similarities between the approach to sports and the approach to school, and those similarities can also hold true in art, music, or any field where students put hard work and sustained effort into practicing and improving performance. One doesn't need to play sports to understand the specific underlying values, just like one doesn't need to be a Navy SEAL to learn accountability, leadership, team-building, and resiliency. While this book will focus on the connection between sports and school, the techniques can be applied to any student who has yet to discover his or her potential in the classroom.

HIGHLIGHTS FROM CHAPTER 1

- Athletic scholarships are rare and limited. We must prepare our students for college without sports in order to prepare them for life.
- If students put the same amount of energy into school as they do into sports, their academic performance can improve dramatically.
- Grades are one outcome of a process, not the goal itself.
- We need to switch from demanding that students improve their grades to finding a way to motivate them to strive for higher grades on their own.
- The ancillary benefits of better grades are the ultimate goal and greatest reward, not necessarily the grades themselves.
- Counselors, mental conditioning coaches, and psychology professionals can be part of a parent's coaching "staff."

CHAPTER 2

WORK ETHIC ISN'T BORN; IT'S MADE

During the preseason of my year as an assistant coach, I had each player write down goals for what they wanted to accomplish during that time. One player (Let's call him "Tim") said he wanted to gain ten pounds of muscle before the season. I didn't want to tell him how difficult that would be (Who am I to suppress someone's goals?), so we wrote up a lifting program to help Tim increase his muscle mass.

Since I had some experience as a trainer in college, I knew enough to help Tim in the gym. On the first exercise he stopped after ten reps. I asked, "Why did you stop?" (When building muscle, it's important to push the muscles to exhaustion in order to reap the greatest reward from each set.)

"That was ten," he replied.

"Keep going," I said. He did three more.

"Keep going! You've got more in the tank." Which he did. This happened a few more times until he stopped at 18 reps and couldn't do another.

"There you go! Nice job!"

This routine continued for several days for each exercise: "Keep going. You've got more!"

About a week later, Tim was running the 600 meters in indoor track. He told me after the race that when he was entering his fourth and final lap, he thought, "Uh oh. I've got nothing left." Then he remembered what he had learned from our sessions in the gym over the past week and the thought popped into his head, "Wait, I've got more in the tank!" His previous personal record in the 600 was 1:37. This time, he ran it in 1:28, and placed first.

During the lacrosse season, Tim and I continued to train the same way. Each day, he would consistently push himself. He felt he was a failure if he didn't win every sprint against his teammates at the end of the practice.

At the same time, as a high school junior, he was starting

to recognize that his grades weren't good enough to get accepted into most of the schools that were recruiting him, so Tim started approaching schoolwork with the same strategy he had learned while lifting and running track.

Each day, he would push himself to study more, to stay more attentive in class, and to work harder on his papers. In the end, his GPA went from a 2.8 to a 3.9 during his senior year. Then he earned all A's during a post-graduate year at prep school and ultimately flourished at Babson College. He currently works as an analyst on Wall Street and recently told me that he still maintains the same work ethic he learned during our time together.

As Tim's story shows, work ethic *can* be learned. In this chapter we'll discuss how work ethic and perseverance (not results) are keys to success, how student-athletes can win in school when they view homework like practice and tests like games, and how student-athletes (or anyone!) can improve when they act like a motorboat, not a cork.

WORK ETHIC AND MOTIVATION

I once asked a client: "What if I could break into the school's computer and change all your grades to A's in high school and in college? What would you do then?"

His answer? "Not much!"

This is how some students (and their families) currently view school. Getting A's is the focus, not the education they receive. The truth is that grades are not what makes someone successful; grades are a by-product of the amount of effort they put into learning. We must recognize that the end game is the sum of what we learn during our formative years, not the grades themselves.

When students emphasize learning, and in turn improve grade performance, they exponentially improve their chances for success. But how do we get them to do that?

The philosophy of education is starting to change in exciting and dramatic ways. Carol Dweck's book *Mindset: The New Psychology for Success*,[5] has been a best seller since its publication in 2007. Dweck helps parents, teachers, and coaches focus on learning and effort, rather than grades. The emphasis is on the process, not the results. It's on learning, not grades; on work ethic, not outcome.

Another pioneer in this approach to education is University of Pennsylvania's Angela Duckworth. When discussing her book *Grit: The Power of Passion and Perseverance*, she stated, "[For] anyone striving to succeed—be it parents, students, educators, athletes, or business people—the secret to outstanding achievement is not talent but a special blend of

---

5   Dweck, Carol S. *Mindset: The New Psychology of Success.* Ballantine Books, 2016.

passion and persistence [called] 'grit.'"[6] Duckworth's book is starting to shape a new model for education. Her philosophy encourages students to create a strong personal work ethic in order to persevere through the tough times and succeed in the long term.

When I first entered the academic/performance industry, I came across a great pronouncement: "A true sign of long-term success is how a student does during their second semester of their senior year." In other words, students who continue to work hard all the way through the end of high school—even when they have already been accepted to their college of choice—have developed the habits and motivation to do well because it's who they are.

We can have a lengthy debate about how to develop a strong work ethic and a growth mindset, but it's not often that we, as parents and coaches, cultivate those qualities in our kids. Instead, we resort to extending an extrinsic reward for the behavior we are looking for—in this case, improving grades. If we offer, for example, a new car to a student in return for better grades, the student may work diligently to earn that reward, but once it is obtained, the motivation is removed and the behavior we were hoping for stops. If a student earns the new car during junior year, what happens during senior year? Or in college? Or in that first job?

---

6   Duckworth, Angela. *Grit: The Power of Passion and Perseverance*. Scribner, 2016.

Here is a fable that demonstrates this point:

> There was once a group of kids playing baseball outside an old man's home. They would play there every day, but one day the old man had enough of the noise and interruptions in his yard. So, he told them, "I love that you guys are playing baseball out here. I will give each of you one dollar for each day you come and play." After a week, he told them that he could no longer pay one dollar and would instead give them fifty cents. A week after that, he lowered it to twenty-five cents. Then finally, to nothing at all. After a week or so, they stopped showing up.
>
> A while later, while in town, he saw one of the boys and asked him, "I haven't seen you playing baseball anymore. Why is that?" The boy responded, "Well, we aren't going to play for free..."

This story demonstrates that when motivation changes from an intrinsic reward (the love of the game) to playing for an extrinsic reward (in this case, money) and then that extrinsic reward is removed, the internal motivator is no longer enough.

I ask this question of my student-athlete clients: "Would you work harder at a job that pays $30,000 per year, or one that pays $100,000 (assuming that both jobs are the same)?" Almost every one of them replies that they would work harder at the $100,000 job. When I ask why, their response is: "Because it pays more." I have had only one client respond differently, and his response was: "It doesn't matter. I'll work hard at any job." (He went on to earn a 3.6 GPA after previously having a 2.3 average.)

As indicated by the response of almost every client, most students have not found this intrinsic motivation. How do we cultivate intrinsic motivation within each individual so they aspire to improve? There is no playbook out there that helps students with this. You try your best to teach them the rights and wrongs, the dos and don'ts, and just hope it works out.

In my approach, however, we need to think in terms of what works best for *them*, not what works best for us. This approach enhances motivation by helping student-athletes figure out what *they* want.

The students who find success are those who learn *how* to work hard. I believe there are three things that lead to success in life:

1. High work ethic
2. The ability to solve problems
3. Intellectual curiosity

In this new world, students who succeed are the ones who have developed a way to solve problems, push themselves independently, and are driven by a defining purpose and personal vision—that is, a vision of who they will be and what they will be doing in the future. Good grades are just a by-product of these ideals.

Let me break these mental skills down for you in terms of sports psychology. Sports psychology is losing the stigma that something has to be wrong in order for someone to seek mental skills training. Once they recognize that performance is not purely physical, many professional and Olympic-level athletes use some sort of mental conditioning program to improve. To reach peak performance, athletes must address the mental aspect of their sport, no matter what it is. As Dr. Gio Valiante (the sport psychologist for players on the PGA tour) once told me, "Sports are 100% physical and 100% mental."

Mental skills training does not apply only to sports. In my book *Thinking Inside the Crease: The Mental Secrets to Becoming a Dominant Lacrosse Goalie*, I describe the "Bring It!" philosophy: "Start building the 'Bring It!' mindset. Let it overcome all your senses. You want them to shoot. It's your day. Bring It!" Having this "Bring It!" mindset helps goalies combat the sense of fear that comes with playing a mentally demanding position.

After reading my book, motivational speaker and author Rob Clark, who wrote a blog post titled "Unleashing the

'Bring It!' Mindset," may have said it best: "How many of us could benefit by embracing that same mindset in our everyday lives?" That's a perfect example of how I get clients to change their approach to school, by taking the mental skills they learn from sports and applying them toward other areas of their lives.

Although this may seem like common sense, it's not necessarily common practice. Over my years of working in the field of high performance, I've realized that most athletes do not have the mental skills training they need to take their performance to the next level. Most athletes call upon what comes to them naturally, psychologically speaking. If athletes can train their minds to think more effectively—rather than focusing on the physical alone—they can improve their game exponentially.

HOMEWORK IS LIKE PRACTICE; TESTS ARE LIKE GAMES

Like sports, the academic setting is an environment in which people are evaluated for their performance. The golfer is evaluated by score. The quarterback is evaluated on passer rating and completion percentage. The figure skater, diver, or gymnast is evaluated on technique and form.

The student is evaluated in the exact same way. Tests, quizzes, papers, and projects are simply individual performances. A small quiz is similar to a game against a much weaker opponent. A final exam is similar to a state championship. Homework is like practice.

It's one thing for students to *recognize* the parallels between working hard in sports and working hard in school, but it's another thing entirely for them to actually *do* it. In the following chapters, you will see different approaches and examples of what works when it comes to changing a student's mindset. As we move forward, we must also remember that this process is about *their* mindset, not ours, and hopefully their changed mindset will lead to lifelong success.

Jared did the bare minimum, until I helped him correlate his work ethic on the field with his grades. This is his story:

> As an athlete, I was naturally competitive and always strived for more. I wanted to run a little faster, lift more weight, or make more saves (as a lacrosse goalie). Unfortunately, prior to meeting with Coach Buck, I never understood how to apply that same mentality to my academics.
>
> Before those meetings, my mindset was that if I got at least a B, then my parents would stay off my back because in all honesty that's really all I wanted. Things started to click for me when I was able to view school as a game and my grades

as the scoreboard. This then led to Coach Buck helping me grasp two concepts: low-hanging fruit and over-preparing.

Things like homework and participation were low-hanging fruit and there was no excuse for not getting all the points possible for those. As for over-preparing, that applied to assignments like tests, quizzes, or papers. I wanted to get as many points as possible, so I would do everything I could to learn everything that would be on the exam and more, or to cover all the key points needed in the essay so that I could get every point possible.

That mentality also helped me to see things full circle. For example, I noticed that each piece of homework or each paper would be contributing to my end goal—so no matter what it was, I had to work hard all the time in order to get that score, thus leading to a good GPA, which, in turn, would lead to more options when I was looking at potential colleges. Once I was able to see how my actions today would affect my future, it changed my perspective and made me want to put in the work at the age of sixteen so I could live comfortably at the age of sixty.

I kept this same mentality in college, applying a lot of the same principles, but I added another significant one. Coach Buck always talked about preparing for a Spanish quiz as if you weren't going to have a quiz, but you were about to spend a semester in Spain and you needed to know the language for your well-being and enjoyment.

I had a tough time grasping this concept in high school, but once I got to college and took classes focused on accounting and finance (which I was considering as a career), it started to make sense. When taking notes and studying, I would often think to myself, "This is something I'm going to need to know for my internship this summer," or "An interviewer would probably ask me a question on this." This wound up being useful because it put an emphasis on the material as something that I would need to know to be professionally successful and to achieve my lifelong goals.

—JARED

FIVE WAYS SPORTS TRANSLATE TO SCHOOL

"Why don't they work that hard in school?"

We are very familiar with student-athletes who put countless hours into their sport to improve their skill, but for some reason won't put that same effort into their classwork. What if they were to view school as a sport? Then they could take that same mindset, competitiveness, and work ethic they use on the field and apply it to their studies.

Here are five basic fundamentals in sports that can be translated into school to help improve academic performance; I suggest sharing these with your student.

1. Show Up!

On the field: Successful athletes show up. Participating in a sport means that athletes must be there for most, if not all, practices as well as games. Excelling at sports, on the other hand, comes down to what they do once they get there. Successful athletes stay engaged by paying attention to the coach, practicing with intent, and being mindful of the objective of each drill.

In the classroom: Successful students go to class—no matter what. Attending each class is essential to improving in school.

Once there, it is up to the students to push themselves—pay attention, do homework with intent, and be mindful of the day's lesson.

2. Set Individual Goals

On the field: Successful athletes have clearly-defined objectives. Even in team sports, individual athletes perform the best over time if they set challenging yet realistic goals to increase motivation, and a quantifiable way of measuring improvement. Those goals might be to start on the varsity team (short term) or play Division I (long term).

In the classroom: Successful students create goals such as earn High Honors (short term) or go to an Ivy League school (long term). By setting goals like these, they can measure on a daily basis whether or not their actions are moving them closer to their goals. The highest performing students focus on the greatest amount of mastery they are capable of achieving.

3. Focus on the Process, Not Results

On the field: Successful athletes (and teams) focus on the task at hand. Athletes improve their performance and lower anxieties by focusing on the next shift, shot, play, or point— living solely in the present. The best athletes and coaches understand that staying in the present will give them the best chance of achieving the results they want.

In the classroom: Successful students stay in the present and focus on the task at hand. Their focus is on the next assignment, as that is the only one that matters. We want students to approach every assignment the same way—giving it everything they've got—no matter the previous grade.

4. Daily Intentional Focus to Improve

On the field: Successful athletes practice with daily intentional focus. Every aspect of a practice session is done with purpose, making conscious choices on the field with clear reasons about why they are there or what skill they are trying to improve.

In the classroom: Successful students study and approach each class with clear intentional purpose. They know spending time without spending energy has little value. Understanding this helps them avoid running on autopilot.

5. Control the Controllables

On the field: Successful athletes focus on the things they can control. Bad weather, hostile conditions, poor refs, opponents, and so on, do not distract them from the ultimate goal. Focusing on the uncontrollables increases unwanted negative emotions and distracts them from executing the present tasks.

In the classroom: Successful students do not get distracted by things that are out of their control—teachers, classmates, subjects, and so on. For students to perform at the highest levels, they must stay focused on the things they can control—attitude, effort, and preparation for each assignment.

Let's get our student-athletes to start treating school like a sport, which is a language they easily understand. This way they can easily make the bridge between working hard on the field and working hard in the classroom.

BE THE MOTORBOAT

I believe there are two types of people in the world: motorboats and corks. Motorboats create the wakes. Corks float around on them. Motorboats have fuel and they use that fuel to get to a certain destination. The fuel allows them to drive toward something. Corks, on the other hand, just stay buoyant. They allow the tides to push them in whatever direction the current is flowing.

During my first three years of high school, I was a cork. I see that now. But during my senior year, I became a motorboat. I was driven to show that dean I was worthy—that I was smart and could accomplish more than my résumé represented. Finally, I had a purpose for earning good grades. I realized that I wasn't afraid of the hard work anymore; in fact, I embraced it.

> Motorboats are driven toward a destination. What are some areas outside academics where your student is a motorboat, and how can you help him or her transfer that fuel toward school?

My goal when consulting with students is to help them find their own fuel that will propel them to another level of motivation and success. When I started my consultation practice, I realized that if I could use what I had learned from my own experience in school, my background as a college athlete, and my formal education in sports psychology, I could help students make dramatic, life-altering changes.

I started consulting with students like Tim, who had the work ethic on the field, and I helped them apply that same work ethic in school. As I took on more and more clients, I became convinced that this strategy worked.

With the help of all the students along the way, I formalized a program, and the results were incredible. Now I'm sharing my techniques with you. Use them to help your student, to gain understanding as a parent, and to formulate a game plan that works for both of you. I have done this with hundreds of my clients, and you can do it too.

How can you take what motivates a student outside of school and use that to motivate them in school?

HIGHLIGHTS FROM CHAPTER 2

- Students who succeed in school have developed the same approach toward school as they use in sports.
- Students who achieve success learn how to work hard and figure out what motivates them to do so.
- Grades are a by-product of a student's effort, focus, and motivation.
- Monetary or privilege rewards aren't effective long-term motivators.
- Students need to figure out what *they* want, and we need to help them figure that out.
- The academic setting is an evaluative environment, like sports. Tests, quizzes, papers, labs, and projects are similar to athletic performances. Tests are like games. Homework is like practice.
- Motorboats are driven toward a specific destination; they have a clear purpose. Corks allow the tide to push them in whatever direction the current is flowing.

HOW TO INSPIRE MOTIVATION

Before we can motivate a student to change, we must consider some contributing factors. It is critical to address where an individual stands socially, emotionally, and psychologically. In this chapter, we will start discussing human motivation using Maslow's Hierarchy of Needs and how it applies to students' readiness to change. Then, we will discuss how you can earn influence so that your student-athlete will be open to new ideas and strategies. Finally, we'll discuss the intricacies of motivation and how you can use that knowledge to your advantage in helping your student-athlete.

(Note: These concepts are not meant for students who have more serious issues like learning disabilities, psychological or social disorders, head trauma, grief, etc. For students who have these types of issues, there are excellent resources out there, and for parents confronted with such issues, I urge you to seek professionals that specialize in these areas.)

ASSESSING READINESS USING MASLOW'S HIERARCHY OF NEEDS

To recognize when individuals are ready to start changing their approach toward academics, it is always important to assess their overall well-being. A great way to do this is by following Maslow's Hierarchy of Needs, a motivational theory in psychology created by Dr. Abraham Maslow. Maslow's hierarchy is comprised of five tiers, demonstrating that some needs (those near the base of the chart) take precedence over others. Maslow states that we must satisfy one level of needs before we can move up to the next level. We start with our basic human needs and move gradually to the highest level of self-actualization, where we understand our own needs and motivations.

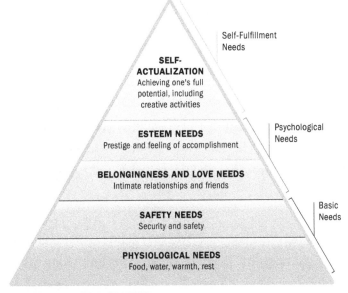

MASLOW'S HIERARCHY OF NEEDS

Students do not need to reach the pinnacle of the pyramid in order to achieve success. But, in the context of school, I have found that fulfilling the lower three levels of the pyramid is critical for students who want to make a dramatic improvement in academic performance. It is important for us to recognize where students fall in this paradigm so we can best serve them as individuals.

According to Maslow, the first (lowest) level represents our most basic needs for physical survival and is the first thing that motivates our behavior. Needs on this level represent food, water, shelter, and so on. Take, for example, a student who is homeless or in need of food on a constant basis. That need must be satisfied first. Once the needs on the lowest level are fulfilled, the needs at the next level must be met, and so on.

As we move into the second level, the requirements are a bit more complex. At this level, security and safety become the focal point. This illustrates the human need for control, financial security, health and wellness, and safety so as to avoid accidents or injury.

If students don't feel safe, whether at home or at school or in the community, it will be difficult for them to focus on anything beyond the need for safety. Recognize that it's what *they* think, not what *we* think. If they perceive a threat, then it's a threat.

One of my clients experienced an unsafe situation that affected his ability to address academic improvement. If this client didn't meet the expected level of performance in school, his father became extremely angry. The enraged father caused the student to feel unsafe, which meant the student's need for security wasn't being met and thus he wasn't ready to address things like motivation in the classroom and improving grades.

Belongingness, the third level, considers a human's need to feel loved and accepted. Humans are driven by the need for emotional relationships—such as with family, friends, and social groups. In short, we have a need to be accepted by others. As you can imagine, a high school freshman's need to "fit in" may supersede his need to get better grades.

It is important to recognize where your student is socially. If he is having a tough time in that respect, we need to address that before looking at the next level. For example, if a child is being bullied or is having trouble fitting in or finding friends, academics may not be her primary focus. In fact, it's likely that the student won't try to improve anything until that need for social acceptance is fulfilled.

Of course, it can be hard for parents to recognize some of these more nuanced social and relational aspects of a student's basic needs. Believe me, I recognize the difficulty of getting answers from teenagers. One idea is to talk to those who know your student outside of the home, such as trusted teachers, counselors, or coaches.

It is not until students reach the fourth level—self-worth/ self-esteem—that they can start making the necessary changes to improve academic performance. Once individuals have satisfied their need for love, belonging, and safety, they can begin to develop positive feelings of self-worth/self-esteem and act to foster pride in their work and in themselves. According to Maslow, "As individuals, we naturally wish to excel or be exceptional, to be noticed for our unique talents and capabilities. Once one has some measure of self-esteem and confidence, one gains the psychological freedom to be creative and to grow, as well as to be more generous to others."[7]

The fifth level, self-actualization, is the level where humans are motivated to achieve their true potential. According to Maslow, self-actualizing people are independent thinkers and are not overly influenced by the general culture. They have a deeply felt sense of kinship. To me, this level is almost philosophical because self-actualization is a lifelong pursuit (The Dalai Lama and Mother Theresa come to mind).

There are five levels of Maslow's Hierarchy. On what level do you believe your student is at present? And what makes you think so?

If a student can reach the highest level of Maslow's Hierarchy, that's great, but it's *not* a prerequisite. What *is* a prerequisite is the achievement of the three lower levels. Students must meet their physical needs, the need for safety, and the need to feel acceptance and belonging before they can truly focus on improving their approach to school or athletics. We must recognize where student-

7   Maslow, Abraham H., and Robert Frager. *Motivation and Personality*. Pearson Education, 1987.

athletes are on this spectrum. If they are still in the first three levels of Maslow's Hierarchy, attend to those needs first. Once those needs are met, we can direct them toward a higher level of success.

Maslow states that lower-level needs must be addressed first. Are your student's basic needs being met? If not, how can you help?

Of course, there are other challenges that students may face when starting this process: They're not ready. They don't believe they can do it. They don't have a good enough reason to change. They don't have time. They'll have to give up their social life. I've heard them all. And we will address all of them in this book.

Is your student in a position to start making major changes? How can you start a discussion about where he fits on the pyramid?

EARNING INFLUENCE

To encourage positive changes in your student's attitude and level of effort, you must inspire, influence, and empower your child to commit to improving her grades. Believe me, I know that's easier said than done, especially when you feel your child doesn't listen to you, or even respect you.

Influence must be earned. It's not enough to say, "Because I said so." You may have already tried that tactic and found that it doesn't work with teenagers. Before we can inspire students to change, we must earn (or re-earn) their trust and understand how to influence them. To do that, we need to learn what motivates them, and acknowledge that what motivates *us* isn't necessarily what motivates *them*.

How do we influence our students so they are intrinsically motivated to start choosing the appropriate actions to earn the grades we always knew they were capable of?

Learning where students fall on Maslow's Hierarchy is important, but we must also understand how to influence students to succeed on their own. One challenge I often hear from parents is: "They just won't listen to me." Before your child will consider a different point of view, you must first gain influence. Then you can persuade him or her to think about making changes.

I know people will say, "Well, you can do that because you're not their parent." I understand that I gain influence with student-athletes because of my experience consulting with college teams and professional athletes, but that doesn't mean parents shouldn't try. Our kids' educations and futures are way too important. In the end, it may take a whole team of parents, coaches, and teachers working collectively to gain influence with students and help them achieve their desired outcomes.

I want to share some advice from world-renowned performance coach Brendon Burchard regarding how to earn influence. I have learned a great deal from him in the overall field of high-level performance, but his particular approach to influence is exceptional. I use his approach especially when dealing with a student who may be on the fence about making a change. (Read more about Burchard's techniques on his website, Brendon.com.)

Burchard states that the number one reason people are not more influential is because they think influence is automatic and episodic: "They should listen to me just because I'm their parent, teacher, or coach." Instead, we need to actively and consistently think through what it is we are trying to accomplish and ask ourselves, "How am I going to influence my _____ [child, player, student]?" or "What do I need to do to relate and ensure that her human drives are met?"

In other words, get into their heads. Find out what's important to them and what they value. Think about this: studies have found that from age eight to eleven, peers have just as much influence on a child as their parents. So, if you're not very good at influencing your children, where is that influence going to come from? Their friends? Teammates or classmates? The internet? Society? The world? What and who will motivate them?

In order to encourage positive change, we must be able to influence others. What are some ways you can earn influence with your student?

UNDERSTANDING MOTIVATION

Although we touched on motivation in Chapter 2, to gain influence, we must have a thorough understanding not only of what motivates our students but also how motivation works. There are two types of motivation: intrinsic and extrinsic.

Intrinsic motivation comes from the things we want to do because we find them personally engaging, fulfilling, and joyous. We do them because we are passionate about them. This is obvious when we see athletes working out or practicing on their own; it's something they truly enjoy.

Extrinsic motivation is the tendency to engage in activities to gain some type of reward, for example, money, power, fame, accomplishment, acknowledgment, or awards. With the crazed recruiting world in today's athletic landscape, many student-athletes are extrinsically motivated by the prestige of going to an NCAA Division I program. They're not even sure what that means, but playing on the highest level—and maybe more importantly, being "chosen" by a Division I coach—validates their performance on the field and can be a very strong extrinsic motivator.

NCAA colleges and universities are organized into three divisions: DI, DII, and DIII. Division I schools are typically the largest universities and allocate the highest amount of athletic scholarship dollars to those teams (not including Ivy League schools, which do not give athletic scholarships). Division II schools are similar to Division I but offer fewer scholarships to each team. Division III schools are the smallest of the NCAA institutions and are not allowed to offer athletic scholarships. There are other requirements for a school to be labeled DI, DII, or DIII, like the number of sports offered by the school, but those are less important for our purposes here.

As a parent, you know what you want—for your children to get better grades or improve their perception of self. Maybe all *they* want is to be left alone. At such a young age, they may not see the bigger picture of how grades and education will affect their entire lives. To help them see this connection, you have figure out what motivates them, whether intrinsic or extrinsic.

UNDERSTANDING HUMAN DRIVE

Internal and external motivators both work. Internal motivators work better for the long term, but external motivators can be the catalyst to start changing behavior. As we start this process, we find a sweet spot in the middle, ensuring both intrinsic and extrinsic drives are met.

The key is to help students find greater clarity about what they want. Burchard talks about the **ten basic human drives** that motivate everyone. It's our role as parents, coaches, and teachers to recognize these drives in each individual so that we can get a better understanding of what's important to him or her.

I want to focus on six of Burchard's ten drives. Deciphering which of these six factors fuels your student's behavior is key to unlocking motivation in school and will give you more influence with your student.

Humans are motivated extrinsically and intrinsically. What motivates your student, in sports or in something else?

1. Control

Humans desire to have more control regarding the outcome and destination of their lives. If we know control is a basic human drive, what can we offer students that allows them a greater degree of control in their lives? For example, I may say to a client, "We know your parents want you to do well, and I want you to do well, but what do *you* want?" When students decide what they want in their lives, they have more control over the outcome, which is very empowering.

Imagine asking your daughter, "What can we as parents do to give you a greater sense of control over your life?" That answer will give her a greater feeling of control regarding the direction of her life. Once she has figured out what she wants, you can collaborate with her regarding how to achieve it. One thing your daughter can definitely control is the amount of effort she puts into anything she wants to accomplish. As Mark Cuban once said, "The only thing you can control in business is your *effort*." Students can control their *effort*.

You might start by asking your child, "What do you want?" This is an important question and not to be taken lightly. It is right here, in this question, that motivation and drive are created—as well as diminished. If the answer is "I don't know," that's okay. Students might not know, but help them figure it out because once they know what they want or what they aspire to do and be, they will then do the work themselves. It will be *their* vision of *their* life, not your vision of what their life should look like.

I worked with a student who was producing content on YouTube. He was very successful in that space. When I asked what he wanted to do with the rest of his life, he said, "This is it. I'm going to do these videos forever." To that, one could have responded, "That's silly," but what we talked about next was the idea of going to college to earn a business degree so he could continue to produce on YouTube while at the same time adding all the skills that he would need to deal with his future successes—things like mastering finances, management, marketing, and e-commerce.

A possible answer to the question: "What do you want?" (if students are honest) may be: "To be left alone." In certain circumstances, that's really all a teenager wants, right? And to earn influence, we need to respect that. If all they want is to be left alone, and all we do is pressure them to get better grades, earning influence will be extremely difficult.

To earn influence, honor what they want. At the same time, help them create an inspirational, positive vision of their future. The key is to recognize that they want *something*, and that they also want to feel *in control* of creating that vision. Then reinforce the benefits of high academic performance in making that vision a reality.

2. Competence

Humans have a desire (and a need) to understand and master their own world. According to the competence motivation theory, motivation increases when someone *masters* a task, which then encourages them to master *more* tasks. The opposite can also be true. If students feel they don't understand school or aren't any good at it, their motivation will plummet due to perceived incompetency. I can't tell you how many times I have heard from students who say: "I can't do math" (or English or Spanish or chemistry...). Our goal is to *recognize* that students may feel incompetent in school for whatever reason, and then help them understand that they *can* do it by staying in the present and working hard. The more knowledge, wisdom, or insight you can provide in an appropriate way, the more competent they will feel.

One of my clients was the top-ranked player in the country at his sport coming out of high school. It is safe to say he felt extremely competent on the field. But the opposite was true in the classroom. He was attending one of the best prep schools in the country, and as you would expect, there were some very smart kids in his classes. He was intimidated to even raise his hand or participate in class discussions.

As it was the beginning of the season for his sport, I asked him to observe the younger players on the field while at tryouts or practice. "What did you notice?" I asked. "They wouldn't even try," he said.

"Well, isn't that just like you in school?" We talked about how he thought the younger kids on the field should respond in that type of situation. "Just try. Put themselves out there. Practice their asses off so they feel more comfortable" (his words, not mine).

Then we talked about how those "better" students in his class were possibly thinking the same thing about him. They probably wanted him to just try because if he put more time into his preparation (studying, understanding homework, paying more attention in class, etc.), he would feel more competent. After that, his grades and, more importantly, his effort, skyrocketed.

3. Congruence

We all desire to feel congruent with our identity—how we see ourselves versus the identity we show the world. If you feel like a lion but act like a mouse, your identity will not reconcile with your actions. So, how can we interact with students in a way that honors and acknowledges their identity?

If they are not honoring their identity, point it out to them. You may say, "Be who you know you could be," or "Are good grades incongruent with how you see yourself?" To build influence, we need to find out how students see themselves, and then help them by challenging that perception as needed. Encourage them to be their greatest self by taking the appropriate actions.

I recently had a conversation with a student-athlete about his current GPA. He said that he had an 84% average, or a 2.9, and that he was putting in a 6 on a scale of 1 to 10 for effort.

I purposefully changed the subject to discuss what college he was considering. "Notre Dame," he said. I asked if he knew what GPA a student needed to get into Notre Dame. He replied, "3.9"—which is correct, generally speaking.

Then we talked about how his attitude toward academics (working at a 6, and thus earning a 2.9) was incongruent with his personal vision of attending Notre Dame. He would need to earn a GPA somewhere near a 3.9, which meant that his effort level toward school needed to be around a 9 or 10 to achieve it. This is a very common conversation when working with Rookies (which we will discuss in Chapter 4).

My client, Emily, is a great example of congruence, or lack thereof. She believed that she was working hard, but her actions didn't align with that belief. After realizing her grades were not good enough to get her into her dream school, she made changes and began to reach her full potential, becoming the type of student she always thought she could be.

Here is Emily's story:

When I first started high school, I didn't really understand that my grades in those early years would affect me so much when I was applying to college. I would keep telling myself that "I'm just getting used to high school," and "It's okay to get a few B's because I'm trying." So, I figured it would be okay to let myself off the hook for my first quarter of high school. But then, I got comfortable.

I realized I could easily get a 3.4 by doing the bare minimum. I would study only the day before tests for maybe an hour at most. I would turn in all my homework but skip reading assignments and anything else that my teacher's didn't check. I told my parents I was trying really hard and that it was the best I could do, but I knew it wasn't and they knew it too.

I was fine with it; I did not want to push myself any harder. I liked my social life, and I liked how much free time I had. I did not want to sacrifice that.

They brought me to see Coach Buck when I was probably in the middle of my sophomore year. I had it already set in my mind that I did not want to see him. I had convinced myself that I was trying as hard as I could because I did not want to change what I was already doing. I met with him once and I told my parents I did not want to go again. I took the easy way out, like I had done for everything that I did not want to do, but deep down I knew I should.

Sitting where I am now, I can tell you that not meeting with him again, and thus changing the way I approached school, was easily the biggest mistake I made in my academic career. During my freshman and sophomore years, I earned eight quarters of straight 3.4's. It was not until I had the first meeting with my guidance counselor about potential colleges during my junior year that I realized I was in "trouble" when I looked at the colleges I wanted to apply to.

All of the colleges my counselor was telling me I should be considering, given my GPA, were colleges I had never even thought about going to. I had always known that I wanted to go to the University of Michigan, but she flat out told me that with my grades it was just not going to happen. That was the moment I knew I needed to make a change.

My parents brought me back to see Coach Buck and from then on, I met with him every week of my junior year. He taught me so much that helped me get to where I am today. One thing that really helped me change was one of his Principles of Effort, "Spending time without spending energy has little value." When I would do my homework or study, I would sit in my room for five or six hours, doing some work here and there but also playing on my phone and watching TV.

I realized that if I was going to do the work, I might as well give it 110%. There was no point in doing it half-assed. From then on, whenever I decided it was time to work, I put my head down. Now, I was truly committed to getting good grades, even if it meant sacrificing some of my social life. This principle solved my first problem of time management and effort in general.

My biggest "aha moment," though, was when Coach Buck told me to "Just play the Sport of School." That helped me see everything so differently. Tests weren't tests anymore, and I never looked at homework the same way again. I just put all my effort into one grade at a time, and my focus turned to the little things I did to score points. If I had a grade that I didn't like, I would just play harder: study longer, smarter, more creatively—whatever I could do.

My 3.4's turned into 4.2's within months. It became almost easy. I established a routine, and knew exactly what to do to make school work for me. Suddenly, I was the person I always thought that I was. As my whole attitude changed, I finally believed I was the smart one; I wouldn't settle for mediocrity anymore because that was not who I was. I finally believed in myself and that was everything.

My new attitude didn't stop at schoolwork. At first, I was scoring 27 repeatedly on the ACT, but then I committed to doing better. Every Sunday for five months, I sat down for three hours and took an ACT. It finally paid off and on my last test, I scored a 34.

I applied all the new techniques that I had learned to my extracurriculars too. I started a nonprofit organization, called Wrapped in Love, that donates headscarves to chemotherapy patients. In twelve months, I had raised enough money to donate over 200 scarves to six hospitals all over the Northeast.

Through all of this, I can still say that although junior and senior year included the greatest amount of work, I still had the most fun socially out of my entire high school career. I didn't spend much more time on anything than I had before; I just did everything smarter.

And sitting here now today, writing this just two hours before my plane leaves for "Move-in Day" at the University of Michigan, I can wholeheartedly say it has all been worth it, and I will bring everything I learned throughout this experience with me on my new journey.

—EMILY

Congruence between perception and behaviors is essential for success. How can you start a conversation regarding how your student specifically sees himself academically? Ask your student if she is being her greatest self—and why or why not.

4. Change

Humans have a desire to change in order to create a greater future world for themselves. We can't progress without change. Paint a better future outcome for students who may not see what better grades can do for them. Show them that putting in the effort will help them tremendously.

Motivational interviewing is a counseling intervention for people dealing with ambivalence (often with substance abuse, but it can be used in other circumstances as well). It starts by asking someone "On a scale of 1 to 10, 10 being the greatest, how would you score your desire to change?"

If you ask your child this question, it is important to collaborate with him or her about how to improve that number, no matter what it is. If the answer is 10, you can then discuss what is holding him back from seeing higher scores. If the answer is low, she may be frightened or have a low level of confidence in her ability to make the necessary adjustments to change. Be compassionate. Your task is to help your student focus his attention on how his current actions differ from ideal or desired actions.

The easiest way for us to help students embrace change is to make a list of things they think they are doing *well* and things they are *not* doing well—along with how they think changing might influence some of those things. Here's an example:

Good things about my current behavior	Good things about changing my behavior
Not-so-good things about my current behavior	Not-so-good things about changing my behavior

5. Challenge

Humans have an innate need to be challenged, and the challenge must be positive in nature. One technique I have tried many times is to ask my clients to give me just one week of working as hard as they can. In some cases, I may only ask for a day or two. Even still, they will most likely see results.

Think about someone who has greatly influenced your life: a parent, spouse, coach, or mentor. One of the reasons that person may have been influential was because he or she challenged you to be great. Coaching great John Wooden (UCLA's men's basketball coach who won ten NCAA national championships in twelve years) challenged us all "to go beyond the role in which most people see us." Wooden famously said, "Be true to yourself. Make each day a masterpiece," which is a great example of him challenging his players. He recognized that as parents, we're all coaches, and great coaches challenge their players. Challenge inspires us. If we strategically challenge our students effectively, we earn more influence.

However, challenging students to embrace a wholesale

commitment toward better academics may make them feel overwhelmed. Rather, break it down into smaller, shorter-term goals. For example, challenge your student to apply herself on one project or test or in one subject, or to commit to an extra fifteen or thirty minutes of study per night.

6. Consciousness

Humans desire to have an elevated experience in the world by connecting to something higher, including activating our full potential. Up to now, the human needs we have been talking about center around the student. Here, we are talking about your consciousness as a parent.

Any influential situation consists of at least two people. When we collaborate, we understand we are going to reach a solution together. In large part, consciousness contains an effort to release control. Coach Wooden relinquished control to his players. He believed it was his job to prepare them for games, and then when it was game time, he just let them play. I encourage you to let your student play, recognizing that you can't control him, but you can influence him.

I understand what I'm asking you to do. You may feel that the situation with your student is already out of control, and that you must take over to dictate her course of action and demand results. However, true change on the part of your student involves change for you as well, and the recognition that, ultimately, your student must make the decision to motivate himself.

For us to help students change their approach toward school, it's important to recognize that we as parents, teachers, and coaches must first *earn influence* over them. Let's face it, there are times when a child simply won't listen to our *great* wisdom, no matter how good it is. If we recognize that influence is not automatic, we must strategically design a plan to earn increased influence over our students and thus create more of a working partnership between student and mentor.

We know a strong personal vision leads to motivation. How can you help your daughter paint a picture of what it would be like if she earned better grades? How can you help your son create a stronger vision of his future?

HIGHLIGHTS FROM CHAPTER 3

- We must consider the contributing factors to a student's state of mind before emphasizing change.
- Students do not need to reach self-actualization in Maslow's Hierarchy of Needs in order to improve academically, but fulfilling the first three factors—physiological needs, safety needs, and belongingness—is essential.

- To help students perceive value in the process, it's important to earn influence.
- Influence is not automatic or episodic, so we must actively and consistently work at it.
- Intrinsic motivation comes from within. Extrinsic motivation is external (fame, rewards, money, power, etc.).
- When students decide for themselves what they want in their lives, they have more control over the outcome.
- Find out how your student sees herself and encourage her to be her greatest self. Paint a better future outcome that comes with better grades.
- Challenge your student to just one week of working as hard as he can on his schoolwork.

CHAPTER 4

FIVE TYPES OF STUDENT-ATHLETES

Now that we've addressed your student's basic needs with the help of Maslow and Burchard, we can start the last stage of pregame: identifying your student-athlete's type. Different factors motivate different students to perform academically—personal identity, work ethic, strengths and weaknesses, competency, self-created limitations, and lack of vision/goals, to name just a few. By understanding your student-athlete's type, you can then implement the strategies that will work best for him.

Based on common behaviors and characteristics I have observed over the years, I have divided student-athlete types into five categories: the Spectator, the Natural Talent, the Rookie, the Workhorse, and the Intellectual. As with

Maslow's Hierarchy, it is important to dive deeper into the type of student-athlete you're working with so we can create a specific action plan for each one. When students apply themselves using guidance specifically for *them*, academic performance generally improves, often greatly.

Students may transition from one category to another, and they may straddle two or three different types at certain points in their academic development. I recently had an exit session with a client who recapped all he had learned throughout our time together. From his perspective, he started his junior year as a Rookie and then became a Workhorse, but desires to be an Intellectual in college. His GPA jumped from 3.1 to 3.9 during the first academic quarter of our time together.

Also keep in mind that each category can apply to sports or to school, and a student may fall into one category on the field and another in the classroom. For example, one student can be a Workhorse as it applies to sports but a Spectator when it applies to school, while another student can be a Workhorse at school and a Spectator in sports. The key is to identify the overall characteristics in both arenas so we can use students' strengths to help their weaknesses.

If you have trouble figuring out where your child falls, ask their coaches or teachers. They will most certainly know how your child approaches sports or school.

THE SPECTATOR

These student-athletes are "Spectators" because they seem to sit on the sideline of their own life. We see this in sports when players are simply going through the motions. They are not pushing themselves on or off the field to improve their skills. They made the team, they are able to spend time with their friends, and that's it. And that's okay. Not every athlete has to be a star or play in college.

Academically, Spectators are just going through the motions in the classroom. They spend little time thinking about how to find success. Spectator students are not particularly driven to succeed, nor are they concerned about failing. They aren't trying very hard, and they make excuses for their lack of effort. These behaviors serve to protect an individual's perceived self-worth by providing excuses for poor academic performance on challenging tasks. The excuses pertaining to school often sound like, "My teacher hates me," "I can't do math," or "That class is too boring."

Inspiring Spectators to perform academically can be quite challenging. They may suffer from low competence motivation and have difficulty mustering the energy to try when they feel academically incompetent to begin with. Focus on helping Spectators create a *personal vision*.

Spectators may have never thought about going to college; therefore, they have no vision of what it would be like. To help these students start envisioning their college experience, I'll show them Google Images of college campuses that are potential fits (usually geographically desirable and a slight stretch academically). Then we'll move to images of football games, or basketball games, or something interesting and unique about those schools. You can also visit a campus; just be sure to go when there are students on campus to make the vision as close to reality as possible. The goal is to get students to see themselves on that campus, internalizing those images, causing them to become interested and/or excited in making that vision a reality.

I once asked a client who was underperforming in the classroom where he'd like to go to school. "I don't know," he said. Then I asked him what type of college program he would like to play for. "I don't know," he said again. Because he had no personal vision connecting him to any particular colleges or universities, it made sense that he wouldn't be motivated to perform well academically because (in his mind), what's the point? It doesn't lead to anything. Without honing in on a very clear personal vision and working toward making that vision a reality, Spectators will continue to simply go through the motions.

If you are working with a Spectator, think about how you can help her create a personal vision. For example, what are some college and universities your student has talked about in the past? What is your son's favorite college team and how can you use that to get him interested in the campus? What campuses could you Google with your daughter? What are three to five colleges and universities you can visit to start creating your student's personal vision?

THE NATURAL TALENT

Natural Talents are an interesting type of student-athlete. As athletes, they amaze us with their God-given skills. Being great at their sport comes easily. Of course, this makes it even more enjoyable. They play with ease, and practice is fun when you are one of the best players on the team. Natural Talents want to play all the time.

But what if their sport was really difficult? How hard would they practice then? Probably not very hard. Natural Talents are frequently the athletes whose parents tell me, "He/She just isn't meeting his/her potential in school." If Natural Talents are good at history, for example, they will complete the work they need to, but in contrast, if they aren't very good at math, they will spend very little time trying to learn it because it doesn't come naturally and requires more effort.

Natural Talents need to learn and internalize the relationship between effort and outcome. If they do, the law of averages tells us they will start to earn better grades and ultimately meet their academic potential. By asking Natural Talents how hard they studied (on a scale of 1 to 10, for example), rather than what they earned on the test, you turn the emphasis to effort.

Nothing will halt a student's motivation quicker than studying really hard for a given test or quiz and then being disappointed with the outcome. If your student-athlete scores poorly after working hard, positively reinforce her *effort*. Likewise, if your child scores well after studying hard, congratulate him on the preparation, not necessarily the *result*. Natural Talents must establish the habit of working hard, so if your child really tries, positively acknowledge the effort, no matter the result.

If you are working with a Natural Talent, think of some ways you can get your son or daughter to understand that work, and not results, is the key to success. For example, ask "How long did you study? Can you try to 'ace' just one quiz? Would you be willing to study for thirty to forty-five minutes?" If your child tries and does well, that level of effort becomes the new barometer for consequent quizzes.

THE ROOKIE

It is easy to recognize Rookies in sports. They are new to the game or to the current level of play, and they are learning the "rules" of that level of play, whether they are a ninth-grader, a freshman in college, or a first-year player in the pros.

Rookies will learn the norms of each organization, such as the repercussions for being late, the level of work ethic or intensity in practice, the attention to details, where they fit in the depth chart, dealing with the media, and so on. During this time, Rookies deal with a tremendous amount of interference, distracting them from what's really important, which is how they play.

Similarly, Rookies in the academic setting are trying to figure out the rules. This usually applies to high school freshmen or sophomores, but I was a Rookie until the start of my senior year. I didn't know the rules, or how my grades measured up compared to my peers, or the connection to which colleges I could attend.

Rookies most likely went through middle school simply getting grades. They haven't spent much time thinking about the consequences (positive or negative) of their academic performance. I once asked a Rookie how his grades finished up for the quarter. He responded, "Really good, B- average." His perspective revealed that he did not understand how a

B- average would negatively affect his chances of getting into the schools he was potentially interested in attending.

What I typically find is that Rookies earn a grade point average that is just high enough to keep themselves out of trouble, allowing them to maintain good social status and avoid repercussions at home. As stated, Rookies usually don't grasp the importance of their academic performance when it comes to their future options. And that's okay. They are still learning.

The frontal lobe of a Rookie's brain—where critical thinking occurs—hasn't fully developed. It's natural for these students to not connect today's actions with the college application process three years down the road. Rookies suffer from the most common roadblock I see in kids lacking motivation: not seeing the connection between decisions made today and the consequential available options in the future.

Rookies need to be told the rules. Show them accepted GPAs from schools they would like to attend. If they have never previously thought about which school they would like to attend, show them the accepted GPAs of some school they are familiar with. It is important that they know what they are shooting for. If Rookies want to go to Harvard, great! But we need to inform them what that entails if they want to get accepted.

If you are working with a Rookie, consider what can you do to show your child the rules and guidelines he or she needs in order to be prepared for the college application process. For example, find out what college programs your child is interested in playing for, as well as the accepted GPAs for those schools. What are the accepted GPAs for Ivy League schools or your state university? Supply your student with that information.

THE WORKHORSE

Workhorse student-athletes stay after practice to drill and work on particular skills they have identified as needing improvement. They are in the weight room regularly in the off-season and after practice. Their effort is obvious.

Workhorse athletes are often Workhorse students as well, taking the same level of dedication, commitment, and work ethic they have on the field and transferring it to the classroom. Workhorse athletes who are not Workhorses in the classroom usually respond to the "play the Sport of School" concept, and this model can be quickly applied to improve academic performance.

The Workhorse instinctively understands the notion of hard work. For example, if you ask an athlete to watch a video about how to hit a curve ball and then go hit one, the

Workhorse knows that simply watching an instructional video is not enough. He understands that after watching the video, he must go out onto the field and practice until he learns how to do it. The same holds true for math, science, history, English, or any other subject. It's one thing to sit in math class and listen to a lecture about how to find the value for x. It's quite another to actually practice that skill through homework.

Olivia is a classic example of the Workhorse student-athlete type. In sports, she thrived on competition and gave her all in every practice and game. Working with me led her to apply her Workhorse attitude in sports to her studies, and soon she was enjoying school as much as sports.

Here is Olivia's story:

> As a freshman in high school, I lacked the right perspective on academics and struggled to get the grades I was capable of earning. Looking back on the beginning of my high school experience, there was a huge gap between how I approached athletics and how I approached academics.
>
> As a lacrosse player, my intrinsic motivation to work hard on the field led to great athletic success. While I was competitive on the field and had high expectations of my play, I lacked this same motivation to achieve in the classroom. If I didn't like a teacher or a subject, I barely paid attention and

immediately wrote off any notion of putting effort into the class. Without the right approach to school, I simply coasted through freshman year with minimal effort and low B's.

This "coasting" changed as soon as I started working with Coach Buck. He helped me to see that academics are as much of a "game" as any athletic event. He encouraged me to treat each test like I would a competition, and to bring the same tenacity I had in lacrosse to the classroom and to my study habits. He helped me to flip a switch; I began to see school as an enjoyable challenge and I brought my competitive nature to that challenge.

I began to notice myself wanting to earn A's as badly as I wanted to win games, and I had never felt that sense of motivation at school before. I noticed myself feeling the "rush" of victory when I did well on tests and projects. Because of this, school actually became fun! I felt significantly more engaged and started to crave the challenge of getting A's.

This led to a change in how I viewed myself. I began to identify as someone who really cared about school and was a good student. It was as if a light bulb had gone off in my head; school is a sport too, and it makes complete sense to approach it as such.

Within a month, my grades improved from low B's to straight A's because Coach Buck helped me bridge the gap between my approach to sports and to school. The sudden change that took place was a direct result of adopting a growth mindset to every aspect of my life, which Coach Buck helped me to realize. Because my academics became so strong with this new attitude, I was able to achieve my childhood dream of attending the University of Notre Dame and competing at the Division I lacrosse level.

At Notre Dame, I graduated with a strong GPA in the hardest major (accounting) from the top-ranked business school in the country. As a freshman in high school, I never would have envisioned this as my future! The shift that Coach Buck helped me to make totally transformed the path that I was on, and it has helped me to achieve great success as a student and as an athlete. Now, as I begin a career in public accounting with a Big 4 Firm, I know that this competitive mindset will be invaluable.

—OLIVIA

Workhorses quickly understand the concept of the Sport of School. If you are working with a Workhorse, what are three ways you can help your student transfer his work ethic in sports to school? Is there something your daughter works hard on for no particular reason other than the love of improvement or appreciating work ethic? In the weight room? At her job? Volunteering?

THE INTELLECTUAL

Intellectuals excel on the field as well as in the classroom. They are dedicated to their studies first, and they will focus on athletics only when their academic requirements are met. These athletes start with setting their sights on an elite school, usually Ivy League, or what I refer to as the "Pachysandra League." (Pachysandra is a plant that looks like ivy, but isn't quite the same.) The Pachysandra League is made up of colleges that are on the same academic level as the Ivies, but they just aren't classified that way. Examples include Stanford, Georgetown, University of Michigan, UVA, UCLA, UNC, Duke, Northwestern—you get the point.

Intellectuals are confident in their academic abilities and see themselves as successful. Their self-image and self-assurance are intact, and the fear of failure does not inhibit them. In fact, they often attribute failure to factors they can control, like poor study habits (i.e., "I should have studied more."). They have excellent study and time management skills. Most importantly, they possess intrinsic motivation and an internal drive to succeed.

Intellectuals have consistently done well in school but may experience negative emotions. What may hold them back is their dedication to perfection, which, at first glance, may seem like a good thing. But the deficit between reality and perfection creates anxiety. Students can become overwhelmed by the desire to do well on standardized tests, or tests in general. They can become hyper-focused on *results*, not learning.

One way to help this type of student is *not* to help them strive to reach perfection or keep their nose above water, but instead to help them lower the level of the water itself. As adults, we recognize that perfection is an ideal. When we are young, we live in ideals because we don't have the experience yet to tell us differently. By helping Intellectuals process what they are striving for and being aware of what holds them back, they can successfully navigate sports and school with less emotional stress.

If you are working with an Intellectual, there may be warning signs that your son is pushing himself too hard. What signs of emotional stress have you noticed? How can you help your daughter keep an even balance between sports, school, social life, and extra-curriculars?

USING STUDENT-ATHLETE TYPE TO YOUR ADVANTAGE

You may be thinking, "Okay, I get the different types of students and athletes. Now what?" Once you have an idea of your student's type, you can use that information to help him in other areas of life. Talk to your student about how she can use that knowledge as a foundation for success in the classroom and beyond.

For example, if your student identifies as a Workhorse in sports, talk to her about how she can use that same attitude to succeed in school. Workhorses already have the desire within them to succeed; they just haven't applied it to their schooling—yet. Workhorses already work hard, so if we can help them apply that effort to school, they will see tremendous change.

If your student identifies as a Rookie, he may earnestly work hard and think he is doing a great job; it is our job to teach him the rules. Few people take the time to look at how this whole college application process happens until the last minute. But if students know from the get-go what they need to earn academically in order to fulfill their dreams, they will be armed with information to make that dream a reality. If they want to go to Harvard and they believe they need a B average to get in, there is no way their dream will become reality.

The opposite may also be true. Your student may believe that only the smartest of the smart attend the best schools, and she may be blown away by the fact that someone from her high school got in with a 3.7 GPA, great essays, and extracurriculars. Rookies must be armed with information.

Now that you understand your type of student-athlete and

the best strategies for his or her success, let's get into my approach for implementing those strategies.

HIGHLIGHTS FROM CHAPTER 4

- Assess a student-athlete's type in order to implement the appropriate strategies for success.
- Over time, students can transfer from one category or type to another.
- The Spectator watches life go by. Spectators are not particularly driven to succeed, nor are they concerned about failing. To help the Spectator, emphasize building a clear personal vision.
- The Natural Talent "plays" sports but doesn't work at them. These student-athletes need to internalize the relationship between effort and outcome. Focus on their effort, not the results.
- The Rookie doesn't grasp the importance of academic consequences when it comes to his future but has a sincere interest in learning and improving. Rookies need information. Review with them generally accepted GPAs for a number of schools, whether academically realistic for them or not.
- The Workhorse works hard at her sport, putting in the extra time on and off the field. Help Workhorses play the Sport of School, transferring their high work ethic from athletics to academics.
- The Intellectual places academics first, but can be

plagued by the pursuit of perfection. Help Intellectuals deal with the anxiety of perfectionism by lowering the level of the water rather than trying to keep their nose above it.

PART TWO

GAME ON!

CHAPTER 5

THE SPORT OF SCHOOL MODEL

After several years of trying different techniques to enhance motivation in student-athletes, a pattern of success started to become obvious. I collaborated with current and former students to uncover what was the most effective process in changing their mindsets and behaviors regarding school. We discovered that the first two parts of the Sport of School Model—understanding consequences and recognizing lifetime goals—were paramount to the initial change. Most students said that grasping these two ideas gave them an "aha moment" and became the catalyst for academic improvement. Once they processed and internalized these concepts, they were more prepared to commit to changing their behaviors and improving their grades.

My experience has taught me that making the transition to earning good grades is different for each student. It's like finding the right combination that triggers a lock to pop open. I have also found that the catalyst for increasing student motivation and improving academic performance is consistently based on the factors introduced in the next few pages. In subsequent chapters, we delve into deeper conversations about why these principles work and look at specific examples of what some students went through on their path to better grades. My hope is that you will find the combo that unlocks your student's potential, and that you can build on it.

UNDERSTANDING CONSEQUENCES

The single biggest factor in motivating students is showing them the connection between what they are doing today and something in the *future*. Athletes who want to earn an All-American status, for example, generally understand the level of skills necessary to earn such an honor. Similarly, students who know they want to attend an Ivy League school understand and accept that their GPA will be a very strong influence on whether they can attend such an elite institution, and therefore will put in the work necessary.

Thus, the first step of the Sport of School Model involves helping students understand the consequences of their actions: specifically, how grades today will affect their future options when choosing a college or university.

RECOGNIZING LIFETIME GOALS

After students understand consequences and take ownership of the consequences of their own poor effort, we can help them set goals for the future. Then we can help them make those goals a reality.

To connect today's performances to tomorrow's consequences, students tend to understand the value of their grades when we work backwards from the future. If they can envision what success will look like when they are thirty years old, it will help them to understand that it would be helpful to get a good job coming out of college. And if they want to get a good job coming out of college, it will help them to go to a good school. And if they want to go to a good school, they need to study this week and next week to get the whole process started.

DECIDING VERSUS COMMITTING

Anyone who recognizes the need for change must *embrace* change. We can all decide to lose weight, quit smoking, or start a business, but actually *committing* to do those things is something else altogether. Many student-athletes want to be all-Americans, but committing to it takes a new level of dedication and a much longer duration.

Deciding is easy. Committing is not. Discuss the difference with your student and try to find something that will create the paradigm shift from viewing school as a chore to viewing school as an opportunity to create success. The "something" that works for one individual will not work with every individual. We must be creative in how we show students the importance of academic performance—until they find that one thing that will allow them to commit to change in the pursuit of excellence.

Once students decide to change and commit themselves to the effort necessary to improve, there are **five main tactics** that can be used to help them achieve their goals. Students will use these tactics in different ways at different times and to different degrees, based on their own personalities, the present class, or an individual situation.

1. WORK HARD EVERY DAY

This part is easy to understand when we talk about athletics. Do a quick YouTube search for "athletes and hard work" and you'll get 649,000 results. It is important to tap into this relationship when trying to sway individuals to improve their grades. I often use one particular video from motivational speaker Eric Thomas. It talks about wanting to succeed "as bad as you want to breathe." The "work hard, reap the benefits" concept is obvious in athletics. We'll discuss how to get students to take this same approach in school. Putting this content on a platform that students are familiar with, like YouTube, can create a path for change that's met with less resistance. In Chapter 8, we will discuss how you can help create that path.

2. FOCUS ON ONE ASSIGNMENT AT A TIME

I came up with the idea of focusing on one assignment at a time while coaching golfers and goalies, helping them consistently focus on *the next shot*. The next shot is *always* the most important. The best lacrosse goalie in the country (on the college level) can only save the ball around 60% of the time. Every shot needs the attention it deserves—it's hard to stop a ball going 100 miles per hour. Whether the last shot went in, missed the cage, or was saved, focusing on it has no benefit. The same can be said for a batter, golfer, or swimmer. The key is to *stay in the present*. For students, that means focusing only on the test, quiz, lab, or project in front of them.

3. PRACTICE MINDFULNESS

Mindfulness is the act of focusing solely on *one's current environment*. This concept has become very popular in athletics as well as in business and overall well-being. If students are to do well in class, they must learn to stay aware in their environment and what they are doing at present time. This can be in the classroom or while doing homework. I encourage some students to not take so many notes in class. If they attempt to write down every word the teacher says so that they won't miss something on a test, they're focusing on the future (the test) at the expense of the present (the lesson). In Chapter 8, we will discuss the value of being present and participating to learn the nuances of each day's lesson.

4. ACT INDEPENDENTLY

Humans have an innate desire to be in control and have autonomy. Academic performance meets those criteria. Students who excel need to feel it is their decision to perform at the level we all know they are capable of. When students decide for themselves to make a change, it comes with passion and motivation. However, if a student feels that improving in school is just something her parents demand, the request for change is met with confrontation. We will discuss how students who feel it is *their* decision to improve will perform much better.

5. ADOPT A GROWTH MINDSET

According to psychologist Carol Dweck, people tend to adopt one of two mindsets. People with a *fixed mindset* believe that whatever talent or ability they are born with is set in stone and cannot be improved, whereas people with a *growth mindset* constantly strive to improve their abilities— physical, intellectual, artistic, and so on. We will discuss how to help students move into a growth mindset, which in turn will help them dismiss their excuses for not being able to succeed in school.

My client, Brittany, now embodies the Sport of School mindset. She was a hard worker in the gym, at practices, and in games, but she had not realized that the same work ethic she applied to sports could be used in school to improve her grades and reach her academic potential.

Here is Brittany's story:

> Before working with Coach Buck, my mindset was to have a strong work ethic, but it was always geared toward sports and what I could do to better my performance and get myself to that next level. This included lifting, running, footwork, shooting, stick work, etc. I knew if I put in the time into all those areas of my game, I would get better and be more prepared. But it never really crossed my mind that I could transfer that same work ethic to my schoolwork.

Sports and school have clear similarities—the biggest one being that focusing on improving the little things can greatly impact the overall outcome. Personally, I spent a lot of time in the weight room in the off-season, and I spent extra time playing wall ball to get my stick skills better. By focusing on the little things, my game, over time, significantly improved. Then, I learned that the same goes for school. If you spend time focusing on the little things, like the homework assignments, small quizzes, or taking readable notes, not only will your grades improve, you will learn more in the process.

Before making the change in my approach to sports or school, I didn't see myself chasing any goals, but once I started to create realistic, process-oriented goals, I became more driven. My perception of self was then altered: I saw myself as a person who was driven and who had a path to follow. I was focused on the process (i.e., excelling at the little things), and in turn, I saw results in bigger things like sports, school, and life.

At first, translating my work ethic from the field to the classroom didn't come easy, but once I started to realize that the strengths I had on the field were the same strengths that could benefit me in the classroom, I began to get better grades and to excel in school. If you consistently work at something and are disciplined in your work ethic, you will see results. They may not come right away, but if you stay disciplined and don't give up on your goals, you will succeed.

Today in college, I 100% still use the mindset that I learned in high school. I still make sure every homework assignment is handed in on time, my goal to get a 100% on every quiz remains the same, my notes are clear, and I start studying days before exams. This mindset of working hard all the time also benefits my athletics—as a starter in a Division I program. Basically, I apply this mindset to everything I do.

The feeling I had after seeing my results was eye opening. For me, it's the same feeling as what you experience after you practice something for a while and then finally get to do it out on the field in practice or in games. Or when you achieve a new personal best in a certain lift in the gym. If you put in the time every day and consistently work toward something, your goals will be attainable.

The biggest "aha moment" I had was on the day when it hit me that I could take the same mentality that I had in sports and translate it to use in school. My strong work ethic was already there; I just needed to direct it toward academics as well.

—BRITTANY

Now that you have an overview and a general understanding of the different facets of my approach, we will get into these areas more specifically.

- The Sport of School Model focuses on three key areas that can spark academic change: understanding consequences, recognizing lifetime goals, and deciding on and committing to change.
- Once students have committed to improving their grades, they can use **five key tactics** to move forward: working hard, focusing on one assignment at a time, practicing mindfulness, working independently, and adopting a growth mindset.
- It's important to be creative in the approach to helping student-athletes to determine which ones work best and become the catalysts for change.
- Understanding consequences and recognizing lifetime goals have the greatest impact on behavior toward academic change.
- *Deciding* to improve grades and *committing* to improving them are two completely different things.

CHAPTER 6

UNDERSTANDING CONSEQUENCES: CONNECTING TOMORROW TO TODAY

When it comes to teenagers and the importance of academic performance, we can find ourselves wondering, "How come they don't get it?" As adults, we fully understand the value of earning good grades, getting into a good school, and how graduating from that good school can impact our careers. But teenagers don't—and it's not their fault; it's biological. They don't have the brain capacity during the early part of adolescence to easily understand the consequences of their actions. The key word here is "easily." They can do it, but the process takes a little longer and/or requires more effort.

Adolescence is a time of significant growth and development

inside the teenage brain, particularly the prefrontal cortex. This is the part of the brain that says, "Is this a good idea?" Studies now show that the prefrontal cortex doesn't fully develop until someone reaches their mid- to late twenties.

Teenagers haven't fully developed the ability to understand the consequences of their actions and then act accordingly. They have difficulty with planning, organization, and learning from their mistakes. For parents of teens, this can be exasperating, but teenagers can still make progress in this area. Experience can play a role in the development of the prefrontal cortex, and children exposed to a variety of stimuli and challenges may develop more quickly.

Since students don't yet have a clear picture of the admissions landscape and how their grades fit into that landscape, this chapter includes exercises to help you quantify and establish just that. Use these exercises to start a conversation to clarify what your student is trying to accomplish and/or what college(s) he or she could be interested in. Then discuss requirements (a certain GPA, for example) necessary to get into a particular college or group of colleges.

USING YOUR UNOFFICIAL TRANSCRIPT

When we show students the consequences of their actions, good or bad, they can more readily see the connection between what they're doing today and how it will affect their future. The single biggest issue I see with students who lack motivation in school is the inability to connect today's actions to *anything* in the future. Which makes sense, right? If a student doesn't see how academic performance will affect her future, why would she push herself to work hard? If students can't see the value of education, good grades, or building a strong work ethic, then we need to show them.

One way to do that is by asking students to get an unofficial transcript from their high school. Most guidance departments can supply one in a couple of minutes.

Without seeing their transcript, most students don't really know how they're doing overall. If you were to ask, "What is your overall and academic GPA?" or "How are your grades?" you might hear the same responses I have: "It's pretty good," or "All A's and B's." When they get their unofficial transcript, however, they often realize their actual grade point average is much lower than expected. (Note: The Academic GPA is the one that includes only core classes. The Overall GPA includes classes like Health and Ceramics.)

Upon learning this enlightening news, students may be surprised or even alarmed. They may experience redness in the face or a sick feeling in their gut. I know; I've felt it myself. What's more, I have found that the students who make the biggest changes in their GPA have had some sort of emotional experience as their catalyst.

For the most part, students who have roughly a 2.8 overall GPA or lower haven't thought about how their performance in school is going to affect their future. Speaking for myself, I didn't realize how bad my situation was until it was too late and had few options. That's why I want my clients to find out their current GPA as early as possible in their high school career. Even if they are incoming freshmen and haven't received their high school grades yet, give them the information they need to clarify what they're striving for and how the consequences of those grades will affect their future.

Reviewing an unofficial transcript can be a catalyst for change. When will you or your student get an unofficial transcript? Write down the date and expected GPA.

GETTING REAL (SPECIFIC, THAT IS)

According to psychologist Erik Erikson, adolescents live in ideals, not experience. They haven't been on the planet long enough to fully understand how it all works, so we need to show them the ropes. This is especially true for Rookies. They may think, "I really want to go to Yale," which is great! I want them to go to Yale too, but you'll see in the table that the average accepted weighted GPA is 100.3 (or 4.53 on a 4.0 scale)!

It's hard to get accepted to those kinds of schools, but some students do it. So why not yours? It's paramount that you help your student understand the academic level they need to achieve to make it happen. Remember, the high schooler thinks idealistically: "I want to go to Yale." The adult thinks experientially: "That's great! But it's really difficult to do."

Students must know the parameters of the college application process if they're going to be successful in attending their dream school, and we need to demonstrate those parameters. If they play a sport, do some research and discover what schools they can get accepted to with their current GPA. Next, show them the average accepted GPAs for those programs.

The averages in the following chart aren't set in stone, but they do provide a general idea of what is needed to get past admissions. This chart shows the top NCAA Division I lacrosse programs and their corresponding accepted GPA and SAT scores. (Note: A weighted GPA represents all of the average GPAs from students who applied and were accepted from a particular high school. A weighted GPA is figured using this equation: GPA plus 5% for honors classes and 7.5% for AP classes. For example, if a grade level math class is equal to 85%, then honors math is 85% plus 5% for a weighted GPA of 90%. For AP calculus, the calculation would be 85% plus 7.5% for a weighted GPA of 92.5%.)

YEAR-END STANDINGS	SCHOOL ENROLLMENT	AVERAGE ACCEPTED WEIGHTED GPA*	AVERAGE ACCEPTED SAT (1600)
1. Duke University	6,697	96.4	1557
2. University of Denver	5,455	90.3	1298
3. University of Maryland	26,922	88.7	1358
4. Notre Dame	7,442	95.5	1485
5. University of North Carolina	18,579	94.2	1485
6. Loyola University	3,807	86.1	1256
7. SUNY Albany	12,878	89.7	1225
8. Johns Hopkins University	5,820	97.6	1505
9. Syracuse University	14,201	89.3	1308
10. Cornell University	13,935	95.6	1446
11. University of Pennsylvania	11,940	99.0	1532
12. University of Virginia	15,595	97.7	1501
13. Yale University	5,310	100.3	1560
14. Harvard University	10,265	97.9	1540
15. Penn State University	38,600	87.2	1272
16. Princeton University	5,142	101.1	1550
17. Lehigh University	4,781	92.9	1338
18. Drexel University	13,980	84.6	1303

*These statistics are taken from Naviance.com for a public high school in the Northeast (recorded as a percentage—not on a 4.0 scale). Naviance calculates the data from applications for a particular high school over the previous five years. It's important to realize that these statistics are just a guide, and not to be treated as gospel. These numbers will change from year to year.

If your student's official GPA is lower than expected (and/or lower than what is typically accepted at her first-choice college), visit some schools that fit her academic profile, even though she may never have heard of them. One client of mine was crushed when after underperforming on his PSAT, he started getting emails from a host of schools he had never heard of. He asked himself, "Is this what it has come to? Are these the schools I have to go to?" The answer was no, but I let him think so...for a little while anyway. Once he realized the hole he'd dug himself into, he made drastic changes.

Discovering his true GPA and learning which schools would accept him (and which ones wouldn't) became his catalyst to change his behaviors and improve his GPA from a 3.0 to a 3.7 each quarter thereafter. This is a perfect example of how to help a Rookie.

Another client found herself in the conference room with her parents, the school psychologist, her guidance counselor, and the vice principal. She looked around as five adults discussed her future and her scholastic options, and she asked herself, "How did I get here?" Her GPA wasn't great (pretty low actually), but her SAT scores averaged around 700 in each section. She was smart (really smart). She simply had not put in the effort to improve her grades.

That meeting became her catalyst for change. She decided

that she would no longer continue the way she had approached school. She took the new approach of, "I am going to prove everybody wrong. I am smart!" Her grades went from the mid-70s to the high 80s.

UNDERSTANDING HOW GRADES AFFECT THE RECRUITING PROCESS

Division I college coaches may be able to help students get into their school with subpar grades, but don't rely on that—every school and every coach is different. Admission to an NCAA Division III program may prove more challenging because DIII coaches generally have less sway over the admissions process than DI and DII coaches.

If student-athletes are considering playing a sport in college, they need to strive to meet or exceed the standard for academic acceptance, thus improving their chances of getting recruited. Without good grades, college coaches of elite institutions can't recruit them.

College coaches recruit high school student-athletes who will likely improve their team, and each year they make recruiting-class decisions based on weaknesses or gaps in their current team. One thing is certain: they know what they need—we don't. From the outside looking in, coaches have seemingly endless options, and their approach is often ambiguous.

However, there is one area that is absolutely quantifiable during the recruiting process: GPA and standardized test scores. These quantitative measures add precision to an otherwise ambiguous process. In that process, academic performance, and not skill, is paramount in both the long term and the short term. No matter what level student-athletes are getting recruited for—DI, DII, or DIII—their academic performance is vital to starting the recruiting process. Every college coach inquiring about a high school player will begin that conversation with, "What are his/her grades?"

Jeremy dreamed of playing for a top NCAA Division I program, but he wasn't connecting that vision to his efforts in school. Showing him how today's grades would impact his goal and tapping into his Workhorse mindset on the field were instrumental in helping him develop process goals that would get him to improve his performance in school.

Here is Jeremy's story:

> During middle school and early in high school, I would get good grades on some tests and projects, but I struggled to consistently string high scores together. My grades reflected this inconsistency; the first two years of high school, I got grades in the low B's. However, with a change in my approach, I eventually found a process that worked, and as a result I earned a 93% average over my last two years of high school.

It all started one day, during the start of my junior year, when Coach Buck pulled out a list of every school that had a Division I or III program for my sport, and next to each school's name was the average high school GPA of their most recently admitted class. As I scanned down the list, I became more and more shocked; my GPA was not even close to being within reach of any of the schools that I had imagined attending.

That was what sparked my determination to change—seeing proof that I wouldn't be able to get into those schools. Up until that point, I had never stacked myself up against the typical admitted student. I had suspicions that it might be difficult to get into those schools, but since I had never seen any proof (or was afraid to see it) on paper, it was easy to come up with excuses of why I could be the exception.

So how exactly did I make the leap forward? I thought about my goals, put them down on paper, and then made sure to attack them in a manageable way. Getting into one of those schools was my goal, but at the same time it had been too abstract and too large of a goal to focus on as I went about my day-to-day activities.

I began to focus on not just getting an A in a specific class, but getting an A on a specific test, and as a result, getting an A in the class and boosting my GPA.

To do this, I came up with process goals that were easily

evaluated, and they helped guide me to my ultimate goals. I thought of them almost as a checklist; if I completed these small things, I could set myself up to achieve a bigger goal.

For instance, if I had a history test, I would write down four or five bullet points on each topic I was being tested on, while setting small manageable goals that had a tangible output (in this instance, the output was a study guide). I found that setting these smaller process goals helped me to block out distractions. It is easier to start with these small goals because they aren't as daunting, and they are easier to focus on because they have shorter durations.

These process goals were instrumental in taking my studies to the next level. They taught me that intelligence is only a SMALL part of getting good grades. What's much more important is a disciplined process that ensures that what needs to get done, gets done. I have applied these principles in many other areas of my life since my high school days, whether in sports, college, or work, and they have been essential to completing my most daunting challenges.

—JEREMY

How can you help your student connect tomorrow to today? What are three ways you can demonstrate to your student what his or her future could look like given bad, good, or great grades?

HIGHLIGHTS FROM CHAPTER 6

- There are biological reasons why teenagers have difficulty planning, organizing, and learning from mistakes.
- Students who lack motivation in school often lack the ability to connect today's actions to their future.
- As early as possible into their high school career, students should get a copy of their unofficial transcript to get a clear idea of where they currently stand.
- Emotional reactions can lead to big changes in behavior and academic performance.
- Adolescents live in ideals, not experience.
- Find out which colleges students will be able to get into with their current GPA.
- Academics are the most vital part of the college recruiting process.

CHAPTER 7

RECOGNIZING LIFETIME GOALS: VISUALIZING A SMART FUTURE

A friend of mine attended a nice, small college in Pennsylvania. Several years ago, she got together with her college girlfriends, and instead of reuniting at their alma mater, they chose the Georgetown area of Washington, D.C., for convenience.

While they were there, they visited the Georgetown University campus. My friend had never been to Georgetown; if you've never been there, it's astounding. The atmosphere is unbelievable, the history is amazing, the cobblestones, the buildings—just beautiful.

After her weekend there, she told me, "If I had known in high school that there was a college like Georgetown, I would have worked a lot harder." Her statement struck me. What she was really saying was, "If I had set my vision on a school with a campus like Georgetown, I would have set goals to make sure I got in." Without vision, we can't create goals—or pursue them.

I suggest visiting Georgetown (or some other similar school close to their hometown) early in a student's high school career. Visit schools that have great academics, facilities, sports, and so on. University of Virginia, Duke, Princeton, University of North Carolina, Stanford, USC, Boston College, and Harvard are just a few that come to mind.

For young students, visiting these campuses early in high school will plant images in their mind, inform them of what to work for academically, and enhance their internal motivation. They will see the options they could have if they put their mind to it. Once that vision has been created in their mind, they can set short-term academic goals that will enhance their motivation and develop a work ethic to make that vision a reality.

In this chapter we'll discuss the need for visualization—the way to set practical, achievable goals—and the power of using process goals to achieve outcome goals.

VISUALIZATION IS NOT JUST FOR SPORTS

One of my clients had a lower-than-average GPA going into his junior year of high school. His dad had finally given up trying to motivate his son and asked me to work with him.

In my first session with the son, I asked him, "So, where do you want to play in college?" He answered, "I don't know." Then I asked him, "So, where do you want to go to school?" Again, he answered, "I don't know."

After that, I understood why he had a problem with motivation—why bother? He had no vision and wasn't working toward a specific goal. He was just coasting along, doing well enough not to fail, but not motivated to work hard.

He and I started to visualize what it would be like to go to big schools and attend football games in huge stadiums, to go to tailgate parties before basketball games with 15,000 other classmates. We created detailed images of what it would be like to go to a great school. While I am a big proponent of goals, I am a greater proponent of a clear vision. (By the way, he earned a 3.9 during his senior year.)

What five to ten colleges can you visit with your student to help enhance his or her personal vision?

If you want to increase your daughter's motivation in school, have her create a vision for her future. Visit a high-end college or university campus, allowing your son to create his own, tangible images. Explain the value of working toward making that vision a reality, rather than simply attending school.

Again, seeing school as a chore is boring. Seeing school as an opportunity to make one's personal vision a reality is exciting, fun, and inspirational.

GOALS: THE STAIRS TO THE TOP

My program director in grad school once said, "There are no laws in sports psychology, but if there was a law, it would be that goals work." I couldn't agree with him more. Once a student has a vision, he or she needs to set goals for how to achieve it. With my clients, I use the staircase theory to help them form these goals.

The staircase theory says that one must know what's at the top of the stairs before we make a plan to get there. Each step of the staircase represents a goal we must achieve to eventually reach the top—our vision. If the vision is to go to an Ivy League school, we can lay out what goals we must achieve to make that a reality: appropriate GPA, SAT, and ACT scores; extracurricular activities; and so on. Or maybe the top of the staircase is to earn High Honors. Here, each step represents the grades needed on tests, quizzes, papers, and projects to get an overall score exceeding 90%.

Discuss the staircase theory with your student. What can you do to assist your son in making the possible vision of his future clearer? What is at the top of your daughter's staircase? What is she fighting for?

Once students have established a personal vision for their college experience, they can set SMART goals. Related to school, SMART goals look like this:

S—Specific: Goals must be **specific.** Saying "I want to improve" is not specific. Help your student choose a GPA or percentage for the grades that he or she would like to earn. I like to use Honors or High Honors as the goal, depending on the student, but I lean toward High Honors first. High Honors is usually 90% (3.5 GPA) or higher. Students may give the rebuttal that they would like to get Honors first, and then try to get High Honors once they see evidence that they can improve. With high school students, I've found that this is a common excuse to get out of pushing themselves.

M—Measurable: Goals must be **measurable.** The goal "do well in school" is *not* measurable. Students need to choose a specific GPA or overall percentage they *want* to achieve—not necessarily what they *think* they can achieve. Making Honors or High Honors is absolutely measurable— you either earned it or you didn't. Another reason I like to use High Honors or Honors as the measure, as opposed to a specific GPA, is that it forces students to achieve a GPA equal to or greater than the standard requirements. If a student makes it his goal to achieve 90% in overall academic performance, he may do his best to achieve it but still come up just a bit short, for example, his quarterly grade might be 88% (or 3.3). By using the honor roll standard as a measure, it allows the student to work hard enough to get over the honor roll hurdle, possibly earning a 92% (or 3.7), for example.

A—Achievable: Goals should stretch your student, but they should also be defined well enough that he or she can still **achieve** them. If a goal is perceived as too difficult to achieve, it will *decrease* motivation.

R—Realistic: For the life of me, I can't figure out the difference between "achievable" and "realistic." I'm guessing that whoever came up with the SMART acronym thought "SMAT Goals" wouldn't have the same ring to it.

T—Time Specific: Goals need to be time-bound to a **deadline.** By setting a specific date to meet their goals, students learn to focus on the day-to-day activities needed to accomplish their larger outcome goal. An example I might use with a client is, "I will earn High Honors by the end of the first quarter."

GOAL ACHIEVING

Okay, so now that we understand how to set goals, let's take it a step further. Students need to be shown specifically how to *achieve* those goals. It's one thing to *set* the goal, but another thing entirely to attain it step by step.

What I've found is that when students see what it actually takes to improve their grades—and possibly make the honor roll—they don't see the task as so daunting. The following diagram illustrates the three types of goals.

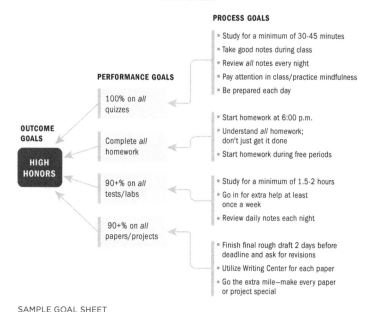

GOAL SHEET

PROCESS GOALS

- Study for a minimum of 30-45 minutes
- Take good notes during class
- Review *all* notes every night
- Pay attention in class/practice mindfulness
- Be prepared each day

PERFORMANCE GOALS

100% on *all* quizzes

OUTCOME GOALS

HIGH HONORS

Complete *all* homework

- Start homework at 6:00 p.m.
- Understand *all* homework; don't just get it done
- Start homework during free periods

90+% on *all* tests/labs

- Study for a minimum of 1.5-2 hours
- Go in for extra help at least once a week
- Review daily notes each night

90+% on *all* papers/projects

- Finish final rough draft 2 days before deadline and ask for revisions
- Utilize Writing Center for each paper
- Go the extra mile—make every paper or project special

SAMPLE GOAL SHEET

OUTCOME GOALS

First, students must establish *outcome goals*. Outcome goals are the end product or final result: to make varsity, earn all-American, or win the championship. In the example shown, the outcome goal is to earn Honors or High Honors. Outcome goals are similar to the overall personal vision, except an outcome goal is just one aspect of how to achieve that larger vision.

PERFORMANCE GOALS

Second, students must set *performance goals*. Performance

goals measure what someone must accomplish to achieve the outcome goal. In this case, if a student wants to earn High Honors, the culmination of all grades she earns should be over 90%—that includes tests, quizzes, homework, papers, and projects.

Quizzes

If High Honors is the outcome goal, the goal for quizzes should be to get 100% on all of them. Is that likely? On every one? Probably not. But the *goal* should still be to get 100% on each one. If one or two is a 90 or 95%, it won't hurt the overall grade very much.

Homework

Since homework is usually about 10 to 15% of the overall grade for each class, students should aim to complete 100% of assigned homework (and complete it on time). When I teach my clients to "play the Sport of School," we discuss that if they want to earn the best grades possible, they need to do *all* of their homework.

Sometimes missing a single homework assignment can be devastating to an overall grade. I'll give you an example: A client handed in all of her homework during the quarter except for one assignment, on which she earned 0 out of 8 points. The problem was that the total amount of points for the quarter ended up being around one hundred. If you took that one missed homework assignment out of the equation, she would have had an A- for the quarter. Instead, she ended up with a B because that individual homework assignment carried so much weight (eight out of one hundred). That's why it's so important for students to complete and hand in *all* homework on time. If homework calculates to 10 to 15% of your overall grade, make sure your student earns 100% on that 10 to 15%. This is an easy way to improve grade performance.

Tests/Labs

The performance goal for tests and labs should be to earn 90% or higher on each. I understand that earning a 90% average on all tests and labs can be difficult, but we are talking about earning High Honors, so 90% is the level needed to be extraordinary. Students achieve it by putting all their energy into the test or lab in front of them.

Papers/Projects

As with tests and labs, the performance goal for papers and projects is to earn a 90% average, but that's actually more difficult to achieve because grading on papers and projects is more subjective. When writing a paper, completing a project, or preparing a speech, your student should perform in such a way that they feel there is no way a teacher can give them anything less than an A. This is similar to earning a starting position on a team. To earn a starting position, athletes must push themselves in practice each day—to a point where they know that they left it all out on the field and gave it their best shot.

Of course, this approach doesn't always work, but the process and mindset going into each assignment should always be the same. By the way, I hear excuses all the time like: "The teacher doesn't like me. That's why I don't earn better grades on papers." And I tell them, "That's on you. What are you going to do to fix it? How many times did you go in to talk to your teacher to make sure you're on track? Did you hand in your rough draft early so that the teacher could make corrections before you handed in the final draft? Take control of your grades, after all, they're *your* grades."

PROCESS GOALS

Third, students must establish *process goals*. Think of process goals as the day-to-day tangible things that students need to do to reach their outcome goals. For each performance goal, have your student write down *three to five process goals* to accomplish each day, for example, studying for a certain amount of time before a quiz or test, going to see the teacher for extra help, reviewing the day's notes from each class, and so on.

Process goals will be different for every student. For example, some students need more time studying than others and others really benefit from going to see the teacher for further explanation. Because process goals are so unique to each person, your son or daughter should come up with this list. It's important for students to feel in control of their grades and academic performance. It's also important for them to feel ownership of the process. If they don't, these process goals will feel like more chores.

FOCUSING ON THE PROCESS

Focusing on process goals will lead to achieving performance goals, which will result in achieving the outcome goal. I have found that when students focus on process goals over outcome and performance, they find the process much less daunting and overwhelming. If I tell a student to go make the honor roll, he may not know where to start, but if I show him the list of the process goals and ask if he can accomplish *those*, the response most often is "Yeah, I can do that."

There's one last thing to do: Have your student write down her outcome goal(s) in large letters in whatever style they like (using color helps). She can write "Honors" or "High Honors" or "3.5 GPA" or some combination of those. Have your student place the index card on the corner of the mirror in his bathroom or someplace where he will see it at least twice a day. Setting goals without writing them down and reviewing them does not count as setting goals. In that case, it would just be a conversation a student once had about goals.

What is your student's outcome goal for school? When will you go through a goal-setting exercise to help your son improve his grades? What are some of the realistic process goals your daughter could incorporate into her daily routine?

Although every student-athlete type can benefit from creating goals and developing a personal vision, Spectators seem to benefit the most. It goes to the definition of what makes a Spectator a Spectator. They are watching their lives from the sidelines; they have very little personal vision about what they want from life and therefore have nothing to act on. If we can help Spectators create a distinct, vivid personal vision, they may start to get more involved with their day-to-day behaviors, and for the first time they may recognize that there is a *reason* to perform those behaviors.

On the other hand, the Natural Talent or the Rookie may have a very clear vision of how they see their future, but often their vision isn't congruent with the actions they are currently taking to make that vision a reality. In other words, they may see themselves attending a top school, but they are not putting in the effort on a daily basis to make that vision come true. Setting outcome, performance, and process goals will help.

HIGHLIGHTS FROM CHAPTER 7

- Visiting campuses early in a student's high school career will establish a vision of a possible future.
- Personal vision enhances motivation.
- Goals make the personal vision a reality.
- SMART goals are specific, measurable, achievable, realistic, and time-specific.
- Accomplishing process goals leads to accomplishing performance goals, which leads to accomplishing outcome goals.
- Students improve more dramatically when they focus on the process goals daily.
- Have students write down their outcome goal(s) on an index card and place the card in a place where they will see it at least twice a day (like the bathroom mirror).

CHAPTER 8

DECIDING VERSUS COMMITTING: IT'S ABOUT EFFORT, NOT IQ

As discussed, helping students understand the consequences of their actions/inaction and encouraging them to create goals and a personal vision are the first two steps of their journey toward improving academic performance. The third step is equally critical: they must fully *commit* to improving their grades, and they must do that on their own.

Alongside our desire to have students put more effort into school, let's keep in mind that we're still talking about teenagers here. Do you recall the self-doubt and confidence issues you had at that age? It's important to be conscious of this negativity as a sort of *background noise* in the lives of many, if not most, teenagers. In my practice, I often encounter students who "believe" they are incapable of doing better in school—to such a degree that even *trying* sounds futile.

So, let's talk about **five principles** I use to help students commit to changing their behaviors toward school. If look back at the Sport of School diagram, these concepts are below "Deciding Versus Committing." In the following sections, I note which concepts seem to resonate particularly well with different types of student-athletes, but all of them have the potential to resonate with any child.

WORK HARD EVERY DAY

As a sophomore in high school, I was captain of the JV hockey team. That might sound impressive, except our JV team hadn't won a game in six years. I learned how to work hard on that team. Our coach was a great guy, but that didn't stop him from kicking us all off the ice during practice one day because we weren't putting in enough effort.

After that practice, I stayed on the ice to explain that I was working as hard as I could. He said, "Oh really? This is how hard you play defense." He then sprinted down to the goal line. Hard stop. Sprinted back up the blue line. Hard stop. Then he sprinted back to me with one more hard stop, and I think he intentionally sprayed me with ice on that one. "That's how you play defense."

I didn't know what to say. All I could come up with was, "I get it. See you tomorrow."

I use this example to illustrate that I didn't know what it meant to "work hard." I thought I knew, I really did. But I didn't. I want my new clients to know that while they might *think* they work hard, they probably don't *know* what hard work looks like. And it's not their fault, just like it wasn't mine.

There is a time in everyone's life where we learn, for the first time, how to work hard. Mine came at JV hockey practice. What's important to understand is that we can project lessons like those into other areas of our lives. A student's struggles may stem from simply not knowing what it really means to *work hard*. It is common for me to hear from a student that they are working really hard, but their parents tell me he or she spends very little time doing homework or studying.

Today I ask new clients a very simple question: "On a scale of 1 to 10, how hard do you work in school?" Over the last ten years, almost every one of them has answered, "6 or 7." Then I ask, "If you were to bump that up to an 8 or 9, what would your grades look like?" They usually answer something to the effect of, "A lot higher." The point is that *effort* is the key to getting better grades, not intelligence. They may think, "I'm just not that smart," but the truth is they're simply not working hard enough. When students believe that anyone can improve grade performance through effort, it reframes what they need to do to improve.

High school is not created to trick anyone. In its simplest form, it is a vehicle to deliver data. Some data is more difficult to process. I once asked a client, "If you only had to take one class, is there any subject in which you couldn't get an A if given enough time?" He said, "No." If that holds true, getting good grades isn't about how smart someone is; it's about how much time and effort they put into it.

We must also understand that student-athletes don't have a lot of time during the day to accomplish all that they want to accomplish. They play sports after school. They have tutors. They have meetings. They have specialized training in a particular sport two or three times a week, and on and on. We must recognize that their time is limited and appreciate that fact. But what if a student-athlete could put more energy into the time he or she *does* set aside for school?

PRINCIPLES OF EFFORT

I help students blur the line between sports and school by using three principles of effort that apply to athletics as well as academics. They give students an alternative way to view schoolwork by correlating hard work in sports to hard work in school.

Principle #1: Going through the Motions Has Little Value

Most athletes understand the concept of "going through the motions." They know when they or someone else is "just at practice" and mailing it in. If someone puts little energy into something, they should expect little out of it. For example, if they go to the gym and don't put much energy into working out, they won't see results. Athletes inherently know that the opposite is also true. The more someone works out, the greater the results.

I realized this effect myself on the elliptical machine: I caught myself daydreaming as I was peddling away, watching the mounted TV or passersby. Then it hit me: I was going to be on this thing for twenty minutes no matter what; I might as well get the most out of those twenty minutes by increasing my focus (mental energy) and speed (physical energy).

Schoolwork is the same. I explain to students that they are doing homework anyway. They know it has to get done, so why not put effort into it and possibly learn something? We know getting great grades doesn't just happen, much like earning All-American in sports. It takes athletes a lot of time and dedication to improve their game. They must put effort into sharpening a skillset to be considered one of the top players in the country. They have to *make* it happen, and the same goes for school.

When I was coaching high school lacrosse, I was in charge of the man-up offense. I'm not sure why they had a former goalie coaching the offense, but I was game. I taught and ran through the plays for about five minutes with the starters.

Then I asked the two players who were standing on the sideline to jump in and get some reps. They both looked at me and said, "We can't. We don't know the plays." This astonished me. They were standing there for over five minutes *just watching* what we were doing. They were not putting in the energy to understand what their role would be if they were called to go in. Basically, they were spending time without spending energy.

What are some indicators your student is going through the motions in school? How can you use examples from sports so your son or daughter understands how to apply the principle of effort in school?

Principle #2: Pushing Yourself Out of Your Comfort Zone Promotes Growth

Athletes who push themselves the hardest are usually the better players. Michael Jordan, Jerry Rice, Tiger Woods, and Mia Hamm are athletes known for their work ethic as much as their performance. It's uncommon for the best player to have the worst work ethic. I know it happens, but not often.

Athletes understand that they need to push themselves out of their comfort zone to improve, but it doesn't need to be overwhelming. Here's the scenario I use to explain this principle to student-athletes: Imagine there is a middle-aged man who is fifty pounds overweight or generally out of shape. If you asked him to walk or run a mile, he could probably do it. It might take a while, but he could do it. Then ask him to run or walk a mile the next day. And one mile the day after that, continuing to run or walk just one mile a day. After one year of doing this every day, could the man run or walk much more than a mile? Maybe a little, but not much.

Let's take another approach to the same scenario. This time the man runs or walks a mile one day, then 1.1 miles the next day, and 1.2 miles the next, and so on, constantly pushing himself slightly out of his comfort zone. If he continued that routine for a year, he would be running over 40 miles a day.

School is the same way. If students continue to put little effort into their schoolwork, they will see the same average results. But if they push themselves to study just an extra ten minutes a night, for example, they'll start to see bigger results.

What are some small actions you could suggest to your student that would push him out of his comfort zone? Studying an extra twenty minutes? Going for extra help? Handing in *all* of her homework on time?

Principle #3: Long-Term Change Is Accomplished through Habits

The third concept focuses on the maintenance of the first two. It's easy to say we are going to change, but it takes willpower and self-discipline to get started. And maintaining that effort also takes willpower and self-discipline.

At some point in our lives, most of us have had the experience of going into the first day of school telling ourselves, "Okay, this is it. This is going to be the year I really turn it on." But what happens? It lasts for about a week. Then we go right back to our traditional ways. To make long-lasting change, we must create *daily* habits that bolster the new choices we have made. Getting good grades is not a sometimes thing—it's an everyday thing. Approaching school in the right mindset must become a habit.

In sports, a good example is practice drills. Coaches make drills a routine part of every practice because they know that drills improve skill. Drills also help the team to focus on the task at hand and prevent them from "going through the motions." Drills cue the mind to think about correct form and perfecting essential skills needed to perform well on game day.

The same concept of routine and practice can be applied to school. For example, students can use the act of walking into school as a cue to remember to be mindful in class. Without that trigger, students will go through the motions and treat school the same way they always have—as a chore. The reward of that chore is pleasing their parents. Does that work? Sometimes. But I can tell you that the students who are working independently to achieve the best grades come to see school as an opportunity to get what they want—more control and opportunities in their future college plans.

At a young age, Tiger Woods planned to be the best golfer of all time. His main goal was to win a record nineteen majors—one more than Jack Nicklaus—so he'd know he was the best ever. To that end, he spent *all* his time practicing and perfecting his craft. In doing so, Woods reaped all the benefits of being the best golfer on the planet—fourteen majors and $88 million a year in endorsements and winnings. His fuel was to be the best. Daily habits helped him achieve his dream. The rewards were a by-product of that fuel.

Similarly, students who get the best grades have some sort of fuel that gives them the energy to establish those daily habits and go get those grades. They may want to go to an

Ivy League school or just ensure they have the most options when they start choosing which college they'd like to attend. Either way, that fuel helps them maintain their focus and effort over the long haul.

How can you help your student create a routine that will help him organize his day after school or practice? What habits can she incorporate to stay committed to change?

WHERE TO FOCUS THE EFFORT

Remember, we are not specifically asking students *to get good grades*. We are asking them *to work hard*. Working hard should produce better grades, but what will be the fuel to get them to work hard in the first place? The key is to get them to focus on their *work ethic*, not their GPA.

Using effort to improve grades works best for Workhorses, who put high levels of effort into each day of practice. They do it in the weight room. They do it in the off season. When we explain to Workhorses that they already have the ability to produce the energy to crush their goals, it is easy for them to transfer that same philosophy to school—because it's already inside them.

The Natural Talent can also benefit from the idea of effort, but in a slightly different way than the Workhorse. Work-horses work. Natural Talents play. We can get Natural Talents to change by asking them to focus on the effort they put into something they don't naturally do well, like writing or math. Then reward the effort, not necessarily the result.

FOCUS ON ONE ASSIGNMENT AT A TIME

In the world of sports psychology and coaching, there is a philosophy that states: teams or individuals should focus on the present to achieve a specific result. Golf psychology stresses staying in the moment by focusing on one swing at a time.

I once asked a professional golfer that I was coaching, "What is your goal today for the tournament?"

"To shoot under par," he said.

"No, the goal is to focus on each and every shot," I answered. "Then, by the end, you'll shoot under par."

In another scenario, I was working with an NCAA Division I lacrosse team who had achieved only two wins in the previous season. After some discussion, we decided that the goal for the upcoming season was not to have a winning record, but to put in as much effort as they could into everything they did: lifting, practice, sprints, or whatever. The team went 9-5 that season—the most wins in the program's history and the first winning record in fifteen years.

In both of these scenarios, the athletes learned to focus on the task at hand. They learned to focus on the present and to give their all in that specific second of the game, round, or competition.

Humans can only focus on one thing at a time; focusing on the present helps eliminate distractions. Similarly, for students to achieve the best grades they can, they must focus on the task in front of them. Every homework assignment. Every quiz. Every test.

I frequently see two scenarios where students become distracted by grades they have received in the past. In one, they earn a good grade or two on sequential quizzes and think they don't need to study for the upcoming test since they did so well on the previous quizzes. In the second, students receive a couple of disappointing grades in a row, and then decide to wait until the blank slate of the next quarter to try and improve, since the current quarter already seems like a lost cause.

In both scenarios, students are focused on past results, projecting those results into the future: "I did well on the last two quizzes, so I don't have to study for the test tomorrow" or "What's the point of studying for the test tomorrow since

I did so poorly on the last two quizzes?" There is absolutely no value in focusing on past grades; students can learn from them, sure, but that's all. There's also no value in using past grades to project what will happen on future tests. To improve academic performance, it's critical for students to stay focused on the task at hand.

I worked with a college basketball player who said he hated to go 0-2 to start a game. I asked him, "Would you be okay if you went 8-10 from the field for the game?"

"Of course," he said, to which I responded, "Ohhhh, I see. So you have to hit the first two to make it a good game?" He got the point.

Another client, Nate, really internalized the concept of "one grade at a time" when I worked with him on academics. He knew he lacked the dedication in the classroom that came to him so easily on the field. Focusing his academic efforts into small daily goals helped him achieve long-term success.

Here is Nate's story:

> Growing up, I knew that improvement in sports took practice, dedication, and hard work. This extra work did not feel like a burden for me because I truly loved sports, and I relished the chance to work on my off hand in lacrosse or run some extra sprints for conditioning.

But when it came to school, I had no idea how to relate the lessons I learned on the field to the classroom. Throughout middle school and early high school, I was mainly a B-average student that never really excelled in any classes. I got average grades not because I wasn't smart, but because I lacked the dedication and commitment needed to be an excellent student.

This was something I heard I could change if I put the time in and did every assignment to the best of my ability. The catalyst for this change came when I started looking at colleges. I knew I needed to do better if I wanted to go to a great school and be a college athlete as well.

So, in my junior year, I started looking into what it takes to be a highly motivated student, and I learned some interesting lessons. A few lessons really stuck with me and I'm sharing them with you now in the hopes that you will use them much earlier than I did.

One lesson that I used throughout college was to take each class one grade at a time. The process of improving your grades does not happen overnight; it takes patience and commitment to try and get better every day.

Imagine that each test or assignment is a game, then prepare like you want to have your best possible performance on that day. This mental switch helped me see the connection between my preparations for a game and how I should prepare for school.

Taking each class one day or one assignment at a time relates really well to another important lesson: take the easy points that your teacher hands out. This refers to things like participation and homework, and even though it may only count as 10% of the total grade, a few extra percentage points may help bump you from a B+ to an A-. Also, completing homework is the best way to help you study for a test or quiz, and it's well known that effective practice makes perfect.

These two lessons, along with changing my mental outlook on school and seeing the consequences of my "bad" grades, helped me reach my true potential as a student. I hope that if you're reading this, you reach your potential earlier than I reached mine.

—NATE

If you can get students to focus on the task at hand and work hard to earn an A on each assignment, they will get a taste of what success feels like—and the euphoric feeling of earning that A can be addictive. Once they get a taste of it, they want to do it again. And if they do, they start to change their perception of *self.* They'll expect more from themselves, and putting in the energy to meet those expectations will become a habit—but they have to do it at least once to get started.

If your student remained highly focused on a particular test or quiz, leave him alone for a week or so. He will feel pressured if you jump on him right away to do it again. If your student didn't stay focused, figure out why. Ask her to try again on the next one.

Most athletes and all student-athlete types will understand the idea of staying focused on one play at a time. The experienced hockey player focuses on one shift at a time. The tennis player focuses on one point at a time. The golfer focuses on one shot at a time. The lacrosse goalie focuses on one shot at a time. The key is to stay in the present, releasing the last play, whether it was good or bad. If students can do this with each class assignment, they will dramatically enhance their chances of improving their academics.

We know the positive effect that staying in the present has on academic performance. How can you talk to your student about focusing on one assignment at a time? What parallels can you draw from the sports he or she plays?

PRACTICE MINDFULNESS

When I talk about mindfulness, I'm talking about more than just visualizing game-day success, breathing techniques, and positive affirmations. Elite athletes and whole sports programs have begun to incorporate mindfulness, meditation, yoga, and other "new age" practices into their training.

Mindfulness is simply the quality or state of being conscious or aware of something. Most commonly, mindfulness is associated with meditation. While meditation may be an extremely powerful tool to reduce stress and limit unwanted thoughts, it is not the type of mindfulness I am referring to.

Mindfulness in the classroom is the ability to stay present. Too often students feverishly take notes during class, making sure they write down everything the teacher says. Why would they do that? They do it to be certain they don't miss any nugget of information that could be on the test or quiz. They are not taking notes to deepen the ideas of the lesson for use later on, in other areas of life; they are taking notes in that way to make sure they have everything they need to earn an A on the upcoming quiz or test.

The problem with this technique is that students are not present in the day's lesson or discussion. Some kids—who are trying to do their absolute best by writing everything down—miss the lesson's underlying message and/or their classmates' responses. In doing so, they bypass what is happening in the present, focusing solely on the future: the upcoming test.

How do we help students become more mindful in class so they can focus on learning and not the impending grade? One technique I use is based on a study from Ellen Langer in her book *The Power of Mindful Learning*.[8] In the study, students were recruited to sit at a computer that displayed colored objects on the screen for twenty-two seconds. The task was to press a button as soon as the object disappeared from the screen, thus recording their reaction time.

The researchers varied the students' instructions concerning how to attend to the stimulus (the object) on the screen. One group was told to focus on the stimulus on the screen and to hit the button as soon as it disappeared. Another group was instructed to trace the outline of the object with their finger. The third was told to think of the shapes in different ways, three-dimensionally, for example. This group was known as the "mindful attention group."

The mindful group significantly outperformed the other two groups in remembering the color and shape. When later trying to remember the shapes, the mindful group required less effort and attention, and they were less frustrated.

You can use similar exercises to help students improve their ability to learn and retain information. Suggest that they become more present in class and think about the material as it's being presented. Recommend that rather than

8   Langer, Ellen J. *The Power of Mindful Learning*. Addison-Wesley, 1997.

vigorously writing down every bit of information, they get involved in class discussion, writing down notes only when they feel the information is pertinent or part of the bigger picture to the overall lesson.

More specifically, at the end of each class, I recommend that students write down the two or three major themes of the day's lesson. The idea here is to get them to see information in the same way the mindful group in the study saw shapes. Instead of memorizing data, assess that data in a three-dimensional way (i.e., "The capital of Spain is Madrid: where my sister spent a semester during college"). As adults we recognize the value of learning and critical thinking versus just regurgitating information we studied on a test or quiz. Students who learn *how to think* (rather than how to cram) will be more successful in the long term.

For example, algebra can be seen as a language to enhance problem-solving skills. The correct value of x is only relevant for the test or quiz at hand, but the problem-solving skill that accompanies finding the correct answer offers value in perpetuity. If we can get students to learn *how* to solve problems—and maybe more importantly, to put *effort* into solving those problems—they can apply those skills in other areas of their lives. Once students see math class as an opportunity to improve their problem-solving skills, they can no longer rely on the excuse: "I'll never need to know this."

All student-athlete types can benefit from mindfulness training, in school and in sports. Mental skills coaches and sports psychologists are using mindfulness training regularly, both with individual athletes and with entire teams, and it will become increasingly more accepted as sports continue to evolve. Intellectuals may see the greatest benefit from mindfulness training, since they tend to experience anxiety about performance. Mindfulness will teach them to stay in the present and let go of the outcome.

Students who are mindful and present in class perform better overall. How can you get your student to be more mindful in class? How can you start that conversation?

ACT INDEPENDENTLY

I worked with a client (let's call her Sarah) who worked hard during her freshman year in the classroom and on the field, but she definitely had more in the tank. Sarah worked hard enough to earn an A- average and potentially play for a Division I program, but she hadn't fully met her potential in either area. Why not? She had been performing to the level of her parents' expectations, but not fulfilling her own destiny. How could I get Sarah to find the drive to really push herself, rather than just meet her parents' expectations?

Our first four meetings during her sophomore year began with the same simple question: "What do you want?" Sarah didn't know...and that was okay. After all, she was only fifteen years old. But in the fifth meeting she finally answered, "I want to go DI."

Once she'd figured that out on her own—that she wanted to go to a Division I school—we could make a plan (athletically and academically) for the type of school she was looking for and take the appropriate steps to get her there. Most importantly, Sarah was taking control of her life for the first time and striving to accomplish what *she* wanted for herself.

Once she'd figured out what she wanted, Sarah pushed herself in the classroom and dedicated herself to improving on the field. I call this "being on autopilot" because she no longer needed prodding. She trained hard in the offseason and raised her grades even higher. She made sure that whoever recruited her, including the Ivies, wouldn't take issue with her grades. (Sarah went on to play for a Division I program at a great academic school.)

Sarah is a perfect example of the Rookie who became a Workhorse. In the beginning of high school, she worked relatively diligently in school and on the field, but it wasn't until she understood the rules of how she was going to get recruited, and what grades she needed to attend some of the schools she was interested in, that she really committed herself to achieving her highest potential. The most dramatic change occurred when she shifted from what her parents expected of her to what *she* wanted.

Erik Erikson believes that we all develop in stages throughout our life. Without going into the details of each stage, the one that's important for our purposes is "Stage 5: Identity vs. Role Confusion (Ages 12–18)."[9] Erikson's fifth stage involves an adolescent's search for a sense of personal identity through an intense exploration of personal beliefs and goals. Up until this stage, development depends on what is *done to* a person. In the fifth stage, however, development now depends primarily upon what a person *does*.

During adolescence, the transition from childhood to adulthood is most important. As children age, they become more independent and begin to look at the future in terms of career, relationships, family, lifestyle, and so on. A child must learn the role he or she will occupy as an adult. During this fifth stage, adolescents reexamine their identities and try to figure out exactly who they are.

One of the most important aspects of my program is ensuring students take control of their own academic performance. Similar to what Burchard says about the human need for control, the students who perform at the highest

---

9   Erikson, Erik H., and Robert Coles. *The Erik Erikson Reader*. W.W. Norton & Company, 2001.

level are those who feel a sense of autonomy regarding their academic performance.

If a student perceives school as a chore to be completed for someone else (typically their parents), they may not develop the intrinsic desire to perform at the highest levels. Let's face it—kids hate chores. If they perceive school to be a chore, they will do just enough to make whoever is forcing them to do it happy.

Here's an example I use with my clients to help them see the difference between the effort they put toward something for their *parents* versus something they do for *themselves*: If your parents are having a party and they ask you to clean up the kitchen and the family room for the party, how well are you going to clean up? Probably not very well. But if you're having your own friends over for a party, how well will you clean up then (If the parents didn't know about the party, the house will be so clean afterward you could eat off the floors!)?

When I go through this example with my clients, they instantly understand the difference between working hard for themselves and working hard because their parents told them to. In their eyes, "Get good grades," "You need to study more," and "Try harder" are equivalent to "Clean up the kitchen."

As I've said, try having a discussion with your student about what *he or she* wants. If your daughter doesn't have an answer, for example, you can ask about what type of college she is interested in. Big schools? Small schools? Schools with major football programs? Southern? Northeastern? Liberal arts? Engineering? Depending on your child's age, she may have no idea, but that may be the reason for her lack of motivation in the first place.

Creating a personal vision about how he wants to spend his four years of college will allow your student to work independently to make that vision a reality. As we discussed with the value of personal vision, we must educate students regarding all the possibilities and let them decide which one sounds best. Remember, as they get older and start to individuate, they need to find the fuel to propel their own motorboat.

Students, as with all humans, want to feel in control of their lives. What specific things can you do to give your student more autonomy over his or her academic performance?

ADOPT A GROWTH MINDSET

Over the years, I've learned that what we adults may perceive as simple steps to earning better grades aren't so simple for teenagers. In the early phases of working with clients on improving their grades, it often becomes apparent that they want to do well but something has been holding them back. We then discuss the value of better academic performance and the positive effect it might have on their lives, but they still can't put it into action.

After our initial meetings, I sometimes notice my clients resisting the idea of putting in the effort necessary to succeed at a higher level. Quite often clients tell me, "I can't do math," or "I'm not a good writer," or "It's impossible for me to do well in Spanish." They have a notion that they weren't born with the ability to understand these subjects, and that they couldn't learn them because they lacked the innate ability to do so. This is a prime example of Dr. Carol Dweck's fixed mindset.

Dweck asserts that people who have a fixed mindset believe that their personal qualities are carved in stone. In Dweck's view, this mindset creates an urgency for people to prove themselves over and over.

She empathizes with someone embodying the fixed mindset: "If you have only a certain amount of intelligence, a certain personality, and a certain moral character, well, then you'd better prove that you have a healthy dose of them... I've seen so many people with this one consuming goal of proving themselves—in the classroom, in their careers, and in their relationships. Every situation calls for a confirmation of their intelligence, personality, or character. Every situation is evaluated: Will I succeed or fail? Will I look smart or dumb? Will I be accepted or rejected? Will I feel like a winner or a loser?"[10]

Personally, I see this most often when students exhibit self-handicapping behaviors and place blame on anything but themselves. They point out how they can't do well in a particular class because the kids in that class are too disruptive, or the teacher hates them, or algebra is stupid.

It is important to recognize that students with a fixed mindset truly believe they are incapable of performing at a certain level. They believe they weren't born with the ability to write, draw, do math, and so on, and it's important to accept that belief as *real*. If we brush it aside and say something to the effect of "get over it," students will feel as though they are not understood, which reduces our ability to earn influence as well as our ability to help. Instead, we need to help students who possess a fixed mindset to incorporate a *growth mindset*.

Those with a growth mindset believe their basic qualities can be cultivated through effort. In this mindset, the hand you're dealt is just the starting point for development. Although people may differ in every which way—in their initial talents and aptitudes, interests, or tempera-

---

10   Dweck, Carol S. *Mindset: The New Psychology of Success.* Ballantine Books, 2016.

ments—everyone can change and grow through application and experience.

Students who have, or who transition to the growth mindset increase their ability to stay focused on the task at hand, even when faced with setbacks. They know that pushing themselves to learn more will help them stay focused on the ultimate goal, instead of getting discouraged by receiving a subpar grade. As Dweck says, "The passion for stretching yourself and sticking to it, even (or especially) when it's not going well, is the hallmark of the growth mindset. This is the mindset that allows people to thrive during some of the most challenging times in their lives."[11]

Students who are fueled with a growth mindset put in the effort necessary to learn and expand their knowledge. They see school as an opportunity. On the contrary, students with a fixed mindset see effort as a bad thing: they have to work hard because they don't "get it" or think they're not smart or talented enough. This belief becomes a constant challenge to their innate abilities.

All student-athlete types can excel more quickly with a growth mindset. Heck, everyone can excel more quickly with a growth mindset. I think there is a spectrum from fixed to growth and don't believe any of us are purely of a fixed or growth mindset.

---

11 Ibid.

How can you start a conversation about a fixed mindset and a growth mindset? Where does your child see himself or herself on the spectrum from a fixed mindset to a growth mindset? What are the specific steps you can take to ensure you are rewarding a growth mindset, and not the results?

HIGHLIGHTS FROM CHAPTER 8

- The concepts of hard work apply to effort on the field *and* in academics.
- Going through the motions has little value.
- Pushing yourself out of your comfort zone promotes growth.
- Focusing on one assignment at a time breaks large goals into bite-sized pieces.
- Learning mindfulness in sports and school allows student-athletes to stay in the present and focus on the task at hand.
- Students must feel they have autonomy to work toward their own vision.
- Fostering a growth mindset in student-athletes encourages change and long-term achievement through effort.

CHAPTER 9

WHETHER STUDENTS THINK THEY CAN OR CAN'T DO IT, THEY'RE RIGHT

I happened to be in the gym after school one day when I was working as a high school coach. One of the girls approached me and asked, "Can you help me with my off-season lifting program?"

"Sure. What's on the list?"

"We have to do a bench press."

So, we walked over to the bench press. Just the bar was on the bench—no weights—and the bar itself weighed forty-five pounds.

"Okay, sit down," I said. "Let's see what you can do." I was implying that she could start by benching the bar alone without additional weights. But then she said something that surprised me: "I can't."

"What do you mean?"

"I can't lift that. It's too heavy."

"Just try it," I said.

"But I can't."

"Just try it. I know you can do it."

Begrudgingly she tried. She benched the bar eighteen times—eighteen times! She went from "I can't" to eighteen reps! What struck me was that before she had any real idea about whether or not she could do what I was asking, she believed wholeheartedly that she couldn't. Why?

Her "I can't" belief about a simple task was a limiting, emotional reaction to how she saw herself and what she was capable of.

Self-doubt—a belief that someone can't accomplish a task— is a constant undercurrent for most of my teenage clients.

It's important to acknowledge how powerful and stifling these negative self-perceptions can be.

All students have a psychological set point that represents their perceived value. This set point will become the dominant neural pattern of a student's habits and behaviors. Over the years, it has become apparent that students' grades are highly correlated with their self-perception. If a student sees herself as a B student, she will get B's. If a student sees himself as an A student, he will get A's, and so on.

It's one thing to ask someone to do something she doesn't believe she can do—like benching a forty-five-pound bar. It's another thing to ask someone to become someone she believes she's not, for example, to become an A student when she sees herself as a B student. That's a more complex situation.

We all have certain ideas of who we are. What is your student's perception of self in school? Do you believe he has any self-created limitations? Are her actions congruent with how she perceives herself?

FEAR IS PART OF THE PROBLEM

The brain is a survival organ. The mechanism our brain utilizes to keep us safe is very similar to the mechanism an animal's brain uses to keep it safe. Just as an animal uses defenses to induce anxiety and suspicion, anytime we feel vulnerable, the survival part of the brain takes over to protect us and keep us on guard. When we are faced with a perceived threat, our brain can slip into overdrive without us realizing it. Michael Gervais, a sports psychologist for the Seattle Seahawks, calls it "the ancient brain that's programmed beautifully to find what's dangerous."

I was working with a student who had earned an 83% average his first two years of high school. We started working together at the beginning of his junior year.

"Do you see yourself as an A student?" I asked him.

"I was just telling my parents that I'm not an A student," he said. "I'm a B student."

"You're not a B student," I responded. "You just put in a B effort." A look of epiphany came over him.

We all have personal set points. Think about what yours are professionally and/or personally. Then, think about your student-athlete. What is her academic set point? A's? B's? Why does he perceive it that way?

After continuing to struggle, he said something that was very telling. He said, "But what if I try, and I still can't do well?" If we can put ourselves in his mind for a second, we can see what he is saying, "If I try and still fail, then I will have to conclude that I am dumb and can't do it." That is why students don't try in the first place.

Imagine being faced with *that* reality. When we are young, trying to find our sense of self, we can find ourselves at a crossroads: "I can stay here where it's safe, that way I can always blame my lack of 'meeting my potential' on the fact that I didn't try. Or I can risk everything by trying and coming to the conclusion that I don't want to face. Ever."

Which will win: feeling safe or feeling vulnerable? The answer depends on how committed we are to change.

If your student is afraid to try, how can you help him or her feel at ease and figure out ways to break through that fear?

Fear may be part of the problem when students are making, or considering, a major change. Many students don't meet their potential because they're scared; they are scared to find out that they *can't* do something. It's your job to help them through this process. Empathize with them and make sure they feel safe.

One way to help students through that process is by approaching change one assignment at a time. Students (especially younger students) see the task of "improving in school" as monumental. You can imagine how the thought of earning a 4.0 or becoming an "A" student would feel intimidating—it challenges their core beliefs about what they are capable of.

PERCEPTION OF SELF MATTERS

Students who make dramatic changes in academic performance do not wake up one morning and say, "I'm an A student, and therefore it is so." They make the changes one assignment at a time, and maybe more specifically, one decision at a time.

To change your child's perception of self, challenge him to earn an A on just one quiz. But, he must commit to it. It may take two hours of studying for just one quiz, but if he commits to it, he gives himself the best chance of acing that quiz. And when he does, he'll know what it feels like to put in the effort and see the results he was hoping for—and is capable of. He now has evidence that he can do it.

Then, ask your student-athlete to try it again. Hopefully he'll get the same results. Then again, and again... In this way, he changes the results one assignment at a time until he has a whole quarter of grades that he's proud of—now he can start to see himself in a new light.

This component to academic psychology was the biggest surprise I found after working with clients for a number of years. I never would have predicted that perception of self would be possibly the greatest variable in academic outcome and that it can be applied to all types of student-athletes. I thought that the inability to understand math versus English, or English versus math, would be the answer. But it turns out that all students can improve; they just need the right mindset, perception of self, and determination to make it through the fear.

HIGHLIGHTS FROM CHAPTER 9

- If students believe they can't get A's, they won't.
- A student's actions must be congruent with their perception of self.
- Set points are the dominant neural pathways that control our behavior, based on expected results.
- Students need to be aware of their personal set points in order to change them.
- Many students don't meet their potential because they are scared to find out conclusively that they can't

accomplish something or can't meet a certain expectation. This feeling is very powerful and it shouldn't be ignored.

CONCLUSION

Students *can* improve their performance in school. You know they can do it. But *they* have to know they can do it, too. This is why my Sport of School Model has worked so well in my practice.

It's easy to see cause and effect in sports: You work harder, you internalize the plays, you show up for practice and give it your full attention. The results come in improved teamwork, in better personal stats, and on the scoreboard. In sports, the relationship between greater effort and better performance seems completely obvious. Why not in school?

The same teenager who's confident and accomplished on the field can struggle with self-efficacy in the classroom. But when students use the same elements they already use in sports to bolster their confidence in the classroom, they see results. As in sports, those results may not be immediate. It takes a game plan, an honest assessment, and practice to improve. It's going to take commitment from both parents and students. And yes, there will be struggles—and that's okay.

We need to honor those struggles. Can you think back to a time when you had to work really hard? When you put your full energy into a certain job or project to make it successful? We often think back fondly to those times, even though it was difficult. Without those struggles, we may not have had success.

Help your child cultivate a vision for her future beyond athletics. Encourage him to believe in achieving his goals. It can't be our vision for them—it has to be their vision for their own future.

You can help them get there with the tools outlined in this book. Here's how to get started:

1. The first thing you need to do is make a plan. In doing so, empathize with your child to understand his or her needs and motivations. Review Chapter 3 if you need a refresher on Maslow's Hierarchy of Needs.
2. Assess which student-athlete type best characterizes your child. If you're unsure, ask coaches and teachers

for their input. Then look at Chapter 4 for suggestions on how to work with your specific student-athlete type.

3. Once you've deciphered your child's specific type and addressed the necessary interventions to success, help her create a personal vision for college (or what comes after it). Remember the staircase theory in Chapter 7: your student can't set process or performance goals if he doesn't have a personal vision and corresponding outcome goal.

4. Explain the difference between *deciding* to earn better grades and *committing* to earning them. In Chapter 8 we discussed five different tactics to raising academic performance: work hard every day, focus on one assignment at a time, practice mindfulness in class, act independently, and adopt a growth mindset.

5. Help your student-athlete define what is holding her back. In the last chapter we discussed how students' perception of what they are capable of is paramount. Discuss with your child whether there is concrete evidence of a problem or issue that is holding him back from reaching his true potential.

My client, Wyatt, is a prime example of the whole odyssey of the Sport of School Model. Wyatt dreamed of playing golf in college but realized that neither his grades nor his golf scores were good enough to get him there. His motivation and vision were there, but his study habits weren't. He was spinning his wheels—going through the motions.

At the same time, Wyatt also struggled with low confidence and a poor perception of self, both on the field and in the classroom.

Here is Wyatt's story:

When I was sixteen years old and a sophomore in high school, I dreamed constantly of playing competitive golf at the collegiate level. Golf was my passion and I liked that being on a team made me part of something larger than myself. At the time, I liked to think of myself as a fierce competitor and a strong opponent, but subconsciously I knew that I hadn't yet become either. In reality, I was an above-average golfer and an average student who was restrained by a lack of focused determination and confidence. As I look back on that time, nearly seven years later, I am proud to say that the decisions I made then to improve myself have had an impact on my life that extends far beyond golf and college.

To earn a spot on a competitive college team would require shooting lower numbers on the course and bringing my grades up. Throughout my high school career, my teachers always agreed that I was a committed student willing to put in the work necessary to earn high marks. However, I always felt like the hard work I was putting into my studies was not translating into results on my report card, a sentiment that Coach Buck agreed with. As we explored causation, it became clear that while I was determined to perform well in the classroom, I had never formulated a plan to actually achieve specific results.

The first thing that Coach and I worked on was making sure I was constantly formulating plans and following processes that were designed solely with the intention of bringing my grades up. It is important to note that this didn't constitute a renewed commitment to working hard, rather it was the process of refocusing my academic hours to the activities most likely to improve results. After running a diagnostic of my study habits, we were able to make strategic decisions that helped me accomplish my goal.

Before becoming aware of the shortfalls in my process, I was like a truck driver that tried to complete more trips each day by driving faster and for longer hours. Then when I was equipped with a tool kit centered around focused processes, I was able to achieve results more efficiently. In the example of the truck driver, this was equivalent to developing a map with more efficient routes.

I would estimate that "playing smarter" accounted for half of the overall bump in my GPA that resulted from my initial work with Coach Buck. The other half was the result of a growth mindset that Coach Buck continued to promote.

As I started mastering playing smarter and my grades improved as a result, Coach and I spent more and more time talking about how much I learned. Coach challenged me to show up at school every day well rested, clear minded, and thirty minutes before everyone else. My goal was then to "learn as much as I could."

The obstacles I faced in the classroom turned out to be very similar to those that had prevented me from unlocking my true potential on the golf course. Overall, my game was solid and my performance in the team's practice rounds always put me at the front of the varsity lineup. However, I still struggled to play my best when things heated up during competition.

I often found myself leading the pack in matches until the final few holes, where I would inevitably make mistakes that cost me strokes. Even more disappointing, I had held the lead in a few conference and state tournaments early on in my high school career but I was never able to finish strong and secure a win at the individual level.

In those situations where I had put myself in a strong position to win, I remember being overcome by the fear of "blowing it again" as it came down to the final stretch. Tee shots that I swung at aggressively in the beginning of the round were replaced by timid attempts to steer the ball and keep it in play. On more than one occasion, I miss-hit short putts because they suddenly felt like three times their true length. Instead of playing to win, I was driven by my fear of losing. Time and time again, this unconscious and emotionally motivated change proved to be a self-fulfilling prophecy.

In this light, Coach and I began to examine my practice habits. On the range and practice green, I was often distracted by previous failures that I would think about while preparing for tournaments. I was intensely focused on the prospect of being in the lead again coming down the home stretch and then focusing only on my fears of coming up short again. This attitude had disastrous effects on my ability to focus deeply on enhancing my skills and also exaggerated the debilitating fear of losing when I was in a frontrunner position.

During my sophomore year, I had been in contention to win on the eighteenth hole of the conference individual tournament. After a nervous and weak tee shot that found the fairway bunker, I had laid up to the front of the green. Inevitably, I was overcome by the fear of losing as I approached the chip shot I would have to hit from just in front of the elevated green. I told myself that if I was just able to get up and down, as I had done without difficulty during practice, I might be able to hoist the trophy for the first time.

As I stood over the chip shot, I nearly became physically debilitated by the thought of letting this one slip away too. As I took the club back, I was already looking short of the green where an errant shot would land and it inevitably did.

Disappointed, angry, and embarrassed, I hit the shot exactly that same way three times.

The following week, Coach Buck made a surprise appearance at practice. He found me on the practice green with a large supply of practice balls gathered ten yards to the front of an uphill green, nearly the exact same shot that had defeated me only days earlier.

Coach stated, "You're a really solid player right now, but you will never be a great competitor as long as you are playing not to lose."

In the conversation that followed with Coach Buck, I truly committed to changing the way I thought during competition and practice.

This marked the beginning of a long journey to start thinking only about the shot in front of me on the golf course and nothing else. I would focus on envisioning the shot I wanted to hit and committing myself to aggressively trying to execute it. After considerable work at this, I was finally able to think about only golf on the golf course.

Just over a year later, I was standing on the eighteenth hole of the Northern Junior with a two-shot lead. I hit a tee shot that I yanked to the left and plugged in a fairway bunker. It was the beginning of a movie that the people there to support me had seen before. However, this time was different. I wasn't keeping my head down because I was too disappointed to make eye contact.

Instead, I was furious because I knew the real reason why I hit the ball into the bunker. Under the pressure, I had returned to playing with the fear of losing the tournament. I still remember my exact thought in this moment, "If you let yourself think like this, you know that you are going to lose. Stop thinking about anything except the next shot and making an aggressive swing."

At that moment, I decided to play to win and a weight was lifted off my shoulders. I pitched the ball out of the bunker and left myself a 150-yard approach into the green. While I had been hearing Coach's voice in my head for months saying, "Sink this," this was the first time I told myself that same thing and believed it. I lined up the shot, envisioned a high draw that went in the hole, and then took one of the most purposeful swings I had ever swung during competition. It landed two feet from the pin and zipped back to ten feet. I sunk the putt and walked off the green the winner, for the first time.

I am sure that many high school athletes will read this story and find ways in which it relates to them. I hope that it will inspire you to think about your attitude toward competition or how you dedicate time to your studies. However, what I want to impress upon you the most is that developing and working on how you compete and how you study in high school will have a big impact on the rest of your life.

If I had not made these changes, I would have continued down the path of an above-average golfer and an average student. Instead, by learning to not succumb to the pressures of competition, and to become more deliberate in my studies and practice time on the golf course, I drastically altered the course of my life.

Unrestricted by the fear of losing, I hit the ground running as a starter on the golf team during my freshman year of college. The pressure of tournament play no longer bothered me; I was just playing golf. I did not realize that I was ranked inside of the top ten players in the conference until the season had finished.

More importantly, the best example of how I translated the work ethic that I developed on the course into the classroom was during the second semester of my sophomore year of college. Coach and I weren't formally working together at this point, but we talked for a few hours every month.

I had a lot of success during my freshman year, especially in the fall. I started in every tournament and I finished the season, as noted previously, ranked inside of the top ten players in the conference. However, when Coach and I talked over the next two semesters, we spent far more time talking about my academic endeavors.

Coach helped me to recognize that the passion I felt for golf was nearly the exact feeling I felt in the classroom. I was studying hard because I wanted to do better for myself. I wanted to win in the classroom and unlock new opportunities. I finished my sophomore year with a 4.12 GPA.

I called Coach and said, "I don't think I can accomplish what I want to in the classroom and maintain the practice regimen I expect from myself as an athlete. More importantly, my passion for my studies has succeeded in my winning conference championships. I think it is about time that I transition to playing golf recreationally."

Coach replied, "I think this is the most self-aware and confident you have ever been. I fully support that decision."

I couldn't help but think about this conversation when I was initiated into the Phi Beta Kappa honor society my senior year. It was clear to me that abandoning the fear of losing on the course had made the transition into other parts of my life. I was now confident and deliberately prepared in everything I did.

—WYATT

I love Wyatt's story because he discusses so many parts of the Sport of School Model. For example, from golf he learned to play one shot at a time ("I would focus on envisioning the shot I wanted to hit and committing myself to aggressively trying to execute it."). Because he had internalized this strategy on the course, it was easy for him to apply it to the classroom.

As with all my clients, personal vision was key for Wyatt, but he needed to find his own way to make that vision a reality. Once he internalized his vision and committed to making it a reality, he created outcome and process goals to help him get there, with concrete tactics to correlate the hard work he put into practice with the hard work he'd put into school.

I also love Wyatt's honesty in confronting his negative self-perception, and the effort it took to overcome it ("If you let yourself think like this, you know that you are going to lose. Stop thinking about anything except the next shot and making an aggressive swing."). Imagine if we could get our students to think this way after a bad grade or a disappointing SAT score. The value is how they react, not the result. They learn how to do it on the field—we need to help them use that same mindset in everything else.

My hope is that if students implement the principles in this book, they will start to see themselves as capable. It won't be enough for students to dream big if they don't believe they are capable of achieving those dreams—or worse, aren't worthy of big dreams. That's where our love as parents and coaches is especially valuable. We must help our students see themselves as we do: intelligent, driven, independent, and successful. We know they can do it. Now it's time for them to know it too.

CONTACTS

To learn more about The Sport of School Academy and Coach Buck, or how you or your student can work with him directly, go to **www.christianbuck.com.**

On The Sport of School Facebook page, you can join with other parents to work together, along with Coach Buck, to help your student achieve his or her potential in school and in sports, and finally see that spark in your student you know is there but have been struggling to find.

For those interested in more in-depth coaching via online courses, Coach Buck offers group sessions with other student-athletes that meet each week and support each other through the challenges of making the big behavioral changes necessary to improve in school. He also offers one-on-one coaching via internet sessions for students around North America.

Visit Coach Buck's website for more information about how he helps Division I teams and business executives reach new levels of success through a uniquely tailored process of discovery and development. You can also connect with Coach Buck on Twitter, YouTube, Instagram, and on the Sport of School page on Facebook.

If this book helped you, the best way you can say thank you is with a great review on Amazon or by sharing it with your friends and colleagues.

ACKNOWLEDGMENTS

First and foremost, I want to thank my wife, Gail, for all her love and support. I couldn't do any of this without her.

I am extremely grateful to everyone who has helped me become who I am today: my parents, George and Dianne, who will love this book no matter what; my mentor, Dave, for always having the right advice at the right time; my editors, for countless hours of review; and Coaches Lars and Jon, for always listening to a new perspective.

I'd like to thank the team at Scribe for having such an amazing hands-on approach to help launch this book—creating a product infinitely better than I could have done on my own.

Lastly, I'd like to acknowledge all of the students and athletes who have given me the privilege of helping them over the years.

ABOUT THE AUTHOR

CHRISTIAN BUCK is a certified consultant, mental conditioning coach, and author. He is the president and founder of Christian Buck Consulting and the creator of The Sport of School Academy. As a human performance consultant and team culture expert, Coach Buck works with sports programs to implement team-specific mental conditioning programs. His clients include Brown University's 2016 men's lacrosse NCAA Final Four team, Amherst College's 2019 men's lacrosse National Championship Runner-Up team, Sacred Heart University's men's lacrosse team, and golfers from the PGA Canada Tour.

Coach Buck's The Sport of School Academy takes the strongest lessons from athletics and applies them to academics to motivate his students to improve their academic performance. The Sport of School alumni have gone on to college programs such as Notre Dame, Georgetown, Villanova, Dartmouth, Michigan, Colgate, and Tufts, to name a few.

He is the author of *Thinking Inside the Crease: The Mental Secrets to Becoming a Dominant Lacrosse Goalie*, which was ranked number one on Amazon in lacrosse books, and *The Sport of School: Help Your Student-Athlete Win in the Classroom.*

Coach Buck holds a master's in sports psychology. He was a guest speaker for Academic Excellence at the Harlem Lacrosse and is a G3 Goalie Camp Goalie psychology specialist. He currently lives in South Carolina with his wife and son.

Learn more about Coach Buck and his consulting work at:

www.ChristianBuck.com
or on Twitter @CBuckConsulting.

CPSIA information can be obtained
at www.ICGtesting.com
Printed in the USA
LVHW110904031120
670566LV00007B/183/J